Ruth and Esther

Back to the Bible Study Guides

Genesis: A God of Purpose, A People of Promise

Exodus: God's Plan, God's People

Judges: Ordinary People, Extraordinary God

Proverbs: The Pursuit of God's Wisdom

Daniel: Resolute Faith in a Hostile World

John: Face-to-Face with Jesus

Ephesians: Life in God's Family

Philippians: Maturing in the Christian Life

1 & 2 Thessalonians: Trusting Until Christ Returns

Hebrews: Our Superior Savior

James: Living Your Faith

Revelation: The Glorified Christ

RUTH AND ESTHER

STORIES OF GOD'S GRACE

WOODROW KROLL

CROSSWAY BOOKS
WHEATON, ILLINOIS

Ruth and Esther: Stories of God's Grace

Published by Crossway Books
a publishing ministry of Good News Publishers
1300 Crescent Street
Wheaton, Illinois 60187

Cover photo: iStock

First printing, 2009

Printed in the United States of America

ISBN 13: 978-1-4335-0661-1
ISBN 10: 1-4335-0661-0

All emphases in Scripture quotations have been added by the author.

Produced with the assistance of The Livingstone Corporation (www.LivingstoneCorp.com).

Project Staff: Neil Wilson

CH 19 18 17 16 15 14 13 12 11 10 09
15 14 13 12 11 10 9 8 7 6 5 4 3 2 1

Table of Contents

How to Use This Study....................7

Ruth

Lesson One: Choosing Grace....................11

Lesson Two: Gleaning Grace....................19

Lesson Three: Waiting Grace....................27

Lesson Four: Not without a Redeemer....................33

Esther

Lesson One: The Silence of God....................43

Lesson Two: Conspiracy of Hatred....................51

Lesson Three: For Such a Time as This....................59

Lesson Four: Dress Rehearsal....................66

Lesson Five: The Bitter Price of Pride....................73

Lesson Six: Courage for Dinner....................80

Lesson Seven: Finishing the Job....................87

Lesson Eight: A Time to Celebrate....................95

How to Use This Study

This study contains the entire text of Ruth and Esther from the ESV; selected passages are printed before each day's devotional reading, so that everything you need is in one place. While we recommend reading the Scripture passage before you read the devotional, some have found it helpful to use the devotional as preparation for reading the Scripture. If you are unfamiliar with the English Standard Version (on which this series of studies is based), you might consider reading the included Bible selection, then the devotional, followed by reading the passage again from a version that is more familiar to you. This will give you an excellent biblical basis for considering the rest of the lesson.

After each devotional, there are three sections designed to help you better understand and apply the lesson's Scripture passage.

Consider It—Several questions will give you a better understanding of the Scripture passage of the day. These could be used for a small group discussion.

Express It—Suggestions for turning the insights from the lesson into prayer.

Go Deeper—Throughout this study, you will benefit from seeing how the Book of Ruth and the Book of Esther fit with the rest of the Bible. This additional section will include other passages and insights from Scripture. The Go Deeper section will also allow you to consider some of the implications of the day's passage for the central theme of the study as well as other key Scripture themes.

Ruth

Choosing Grace

As you study this lesson, notice how determined Ruth was when she decided to follow Naomi and embrace God as her own. Think back to when you first decided to leave your old life and follow Christ. Ask yourself if you have set your heart to follow Christ with the same resolve that Ruth possessed when she fixed her mind and feet to follow Naomi.

Ruth 1

Naomi Widowed

1 In the days when the judges ruled
there was a famine in the land, and
a man of Bethlehem in Judah went to
sojourn in the country of Moab, he and
his wife and his two sons. 2The name of
the man was Elimelech and the name
of his wife Naomi, and the names of
his two sons were Mahlon and Chilion.
They were Ephrathites from Bethlehem
in Judah. They went into the country
of Moab and remained there. 3But
Elimelech, the husband of Naomi, died,
and she was left with her two sons.
4These took Moabite wives; the name
of the one was Orpah and the name of
the other Ruth. They lived there about
ten years, 5and both Mahlon and Chilion
died, so that the woman was left without
her two sons and her husband.

Key Verse

But Ruth said, "Do not urge me to leave you or to return from following you. For where you go I will go, and where you lodge I will lodge. Your people shall be my people, and your God my God. Where you die I will die, and there will I be buried. May the LORD *do so to me and more also if anything but death parts me from you"* (Ruth 1:16–17).

Ruth's Loyalty to Naomi

6Then she arose with her daughters-in-
law to return from the country of Moab,
for she had heard in the fields of Moab
that the LORD had visited his people and
given them food. 7So she set out from
the place where she was with her two
daughters-in-law, and they went on the
way to return to the land of Judah. 8But
Naomi said to her two daughters-in-law,
"Go, return each of you to her mother's
house. May the LORD deal kindly with
you, as you have dealt with the dead
and with me. 9The LORD grant that you
may find rest, each of you in the house
of her husband!" Then she kissed them,
and they lifted up their voices and wept.
10And they said to her, "No, we will return
with you to your people." 11But Naomi
said, "Turn back, my daughters; why
will you go with me? Have I yet sons in
my womb that they may become your
husbands? 12Turn back, my daughters;
go your way, for I am too old to have a
husband. If I should say I have hope,
even if I should have a husband this
night and should bear sons, 13would
you therefore wait till they were grown?
Would you therefore refrain from
marrying? No, my daughters, for it is
exceedingly bitter to me for your sake
that the hand of the LORD has gone out
against me." 14Then they lifted up their
voices and wept again. And Orpah kissed
her mother-in-law, but Ruth clung to her.

15And she said, "See, your sister-in-law
has gone back to her people and to her
gods; return after your sister-in-law."
16But Ruth said, "Do not urge me to leave
you or to return from following you. For
where you go I will go, and where you
lodge I will lodge. Your people shall
be my people, and your God my God.
17Where you die I will die, and there will I
be buried. May the LORD do so to me and
more also if anything but death parts me
from you." 18And when Naomi saw that
she was determined to go with her, she
said no more.

Naomi and Ruth Return

[19]So the two of them went on until
they came to Bethlehem. And when they
came to Bethlehem, the whole town
was stirred because of them. And the
women said, "Is this Naomi?" [20]She said
to them, "Do not call me Naomi; call me
Mara, for the Almighty has dealt very
bitterly with me. [21]I went away full, and
the Lord has brought me back empty.
Why call me Naomi, when the Lord has
testified against me and the Almighty
has brought calamity upon me?"

[22]So Naomi returned, and Ruth the
Moabite her daughter-in-law with her,
who returned from the country of Moab.
And they came to Bethlehem at the
beginning of barley harvest.

Go Deeper

The story of Ruth is an amazing account of God's grace in Ruth's life. The very fact that God chooses us and gives us the privilege of choosing His way is evidence of His grace toward us as well. Let's look at some evidences of God's grace in Ruth's life here in the first chapter of Ruth.

1. She married into a Hebrew family who knew the true God and demonstrated faith in such a way that Ruth was drawn to Him.

2. When Ruth faced the choice to go on to Judah or turn back, God led Ruth to make the best choices—the choice to leave Moab and follow her mother-in-law and the choice to receive Naomi's God as her God.

3. Ruth arrived in Judah at the time of the barley harvest. God enabled her to gather grain to sustain life for herself and her mother-in-law.

4. God gave Ruth the humility and courage to follow Naomi's instructions and approach Boaz.

As you study Ruth and Esther and take note of God's grace in their lives, pray that you become more and more aware of His grace in your life.

The beginning words of the Book of Ruth introduce us to Naomi: Ruth's mother-in-law, an Israelite who left Judah during a famine and migrated with her husband and two sons to Moab. While the family lived in that Gentile nation, Naomi's sons married Moabite women. But the day came when Naomi found herself alone (except for daughters-in-law) in a land not her own: Her husband and sons had died.

So, she made a decision to head home to Judah. Her daughter-in-law, Ruth, determined to go with Naomi. It was during that journey that Ruth said the powerful words in today's key verses to her mother-in-law. They were expressions of love, commitment, and faith spoken when Naomi urged Ruth to turn back to Moab. These words in 1:16–17 are the centerpiece of the Book of Ruth. Ruth chose Judah and life with her mother-in-law instead of turning back to Moab. Why did she make that choice?

Ruth 4:15 tells us that she loved her mother-in-law. It was also likely that Naomi's relationship with God made an impact on Ruth: Ruth had witnessed Naomi's devotion to her God during the most difficult days of her life, days when she'd lost her husband and sons. Ruth's spirit had been drawn to the true God during her years as part of Naomi's family.

So, she made a decision that would affect the rest of her life—both earthly and eternal. She chose to become a new person, a citizen in a new land, a believer in the God of Israel. That made all the difference in her life. When we choose to follow Christ, it makes all the difference in our lives too.

This lesson's key verses are likely very familiar to you. But read them again out loud. Examine the three-part commitment Ruth made to her mother-in-law. Do you see the similarities to the commitment we make to Jesus when we receive His salvation?

First she said, "Where you go I will go." For Ruth, that meant accompanying Naomi to Judah. It meant traveling with her, walking where Naomi walked for the rest of her life. For us, it means following Jesus anywhere He might lead us. It means obedience to God's Word and the directions He provides as we walk through life with Him. Jesus makes it clear in John 14:21 that through obedience we

"When we become new creatures in Christ Jesus, rather than following other gods (such as selfish desires or materialism), we are making a choice and declaring that we will follow the God of the Bible. And that's good news, because as newly-changed creatures, with Christ living in us, new experiences and spiritual growth are endless."

demonstrate our love to Him: "Whoever has my commandments and keeps them, he it is who loves me." It means an attitude of complete surrender to His way—His path. That's the attitude He expects of us when we choose to follow Christ. The disciples of Jesus demonstrated the same attitude. Jesus said to Andrew, "Follow me, and I will make you fishers of men" (Matt. 4:19), and Andrew followed. Like the disciples, we don't have to know the way; we just have to follow the Savior.

The second commitment Ruth made to Naomi was, "Where you lodge I will lodge." In this statement, Ruth revealed her willingness to step into new surroundings and adopt new behaviors. When we commit to Jesus, He calls us to leave our comfort zones—the familiar, comfortable, easy path we'd like to travel—and follow Him. That's not always an attractive prospect.

Matthew 8:19–20 tells us, "And a scribe came up and said to him, 'Teacher, I will follow you wherever you go.' And Jesus said to him, 'Foxes have holes, and birds of the air have nests, but the Son of Man has nowhere to lay his head.'"

In other words, Jesus said, "It won't be easy." We might not want to go where Jesus leads us because it doesn't make us comfortable; it's not the easiest path. We might be required to act in ways that are unselfish; we might have to be humble, show loyalty, and work hard just like Ruth did. We may have to forgive people who have really hurt us, extend compassion to a nasty, difficult relative, or give to someone in need rather than buying that new laptop we want. But since He's already gone before us and promises to be with us, we only have to trust Him and say, "Wherever you lodge I will lodge"—even if there's nowhere to lay my head.

The third part of Ruth's commitment was, "Your people shall be my people, and your God my God." When we choose to follow Jesus, we become new creatures in Christ. We become part of the family of God. We're called to leave our former identities behind. Often, it means we lose some friends who don't appreciate our new lifestyle. But just as Ruth could not become a follower of God without leaving behind her pagan country and customs, we must leave behind our familiar, sinful haunts and hangouts. We're called to a new life.

This new life involves new people and new customs, just as it did for Ruth. In the family of God, we are called to love and serve one another so that we can show His love to the world. "By this all people will know that you are my disciples, if you have love for one another" (John 13:35).

Thankfully, the Bible is filled with instructions on what that looks like. It involves living in harmony (Rom.15:5; 1 Cor. 12:25; 2 Cor. 13:11); serving others (John 13:14; Gal. 5:13); and instructing one another (Rom. 15:14). Most of all, it involves commitment to the people Jesus holds dear: "Let us hold fast the confession of our hope without wavering, for he who promised is faithful. And let us consider how to stir up one another to love and good works, not neglecting to meet together, as is the habit of some, but encouraging one another, and all the more as you see the Day drawing near" (Heb. 10:23–25).

But the third commitment doesn't end with people. Read again the last part of Ruth's statement: "And your God my God." This was Ruth's biggest step. She was renouncing her gods and receiving Naomi's God. When we join a new family, it always requires some adjustments. But when we become new creatures in Christ Jesus, rather than following other gods (such as selfish desires or materialism), we are making a choice and declaring that we will follow the God of the Bible. And that's good news, because as newly-changed creatures, with Christ living in us, new experiences and spiritual growth are endless.

Express It

Think about choices you have made that have impacted your destiny. Did you realize at the time you were making a life-altering decision? Draw a line to represent your life since you accepted Christ. Then mark the major decisions you've made since that choice. On one side of the line, note how you responded to that decision; on the other side, note how you think you would have responded before you began to follow Christ. Thank God for the difference He's made in your life.

Consider It

As you read Ruth 1, consider these questions:

1) Why did Naomi decide to return to Judah?

2) Examine Naomi's exchange with her daughters-in-law in verses 8–18. Why did Naomi want her daughters-in-law to return to Moab?

3) What made Naomi stop urging Ruth to return to the land of her upbringing?

4) On what occasions have you left your comfort zone to follow Jesus' leading? Is God asking you to step out of a comfort zone today?

5) Naomi and Ruth returned to Bethlehem in Judah in verse 19 and the town was "stirred because of them." What might be some reasons for this reaction?

6) Compare the name "Naomi" (meaning "pleasant") with the self-inflicted name "Mara" (which means "bitter"). What does Naomi's response in verse 20 tell you about her state of mind?

7) Naomi and Ruth arrived in Bethlehem at the beginning of what season (v. 22)? What might be the significance of this?

8) What examples of God's grace do you see in Ruth 1?

Gleaning Grace

How long has it been since you thought about God's grace in your life? Think about it now. Think of at least four specific times that you recognized God's grace in your life.

Ruth 2

Key Verse

Now Naomi had a relative of her husband's, a worthy man of the clan of Elimelech, whose name was Boaz (Ruth 2:1).

Ruth Meets Boaz

2 Now Naomi had a relative of her husband's, a worthy man of the clan of Elimelech, whose name was Boaz. 2And Ruth the Moabite said to Naomi, "Let me go to the field and glean among the ears of grain after him in whose sight I shall find favor." And she said to her, "Go, my daughter." 3So she set out and went and gleaned in the field after the reapers, and she happened to come to the part of the field belonging to Boaz, who was of the clan of Elimelech. 4And behold, Boaz came from Bethlehem. And he said to the reapers, "The LORD be with you!" And they answered, "The LORD bless you." 5Then Boaz said to his young man who was in charge of the reapers, "Whose young woman is this?" 6And the servant who was in charge of the reapers answered, "She is the young Moabite woman, who came back with Naomi from the country of Moab. 7She said, 'Please let me glean and gather among the sheaves after the reapers.'So she came, and she has continued from early morning until now, except for a short rest."

8Then Boaz said to Ruth, "Now, listen, my daughter, do not go to glean in another field or leave this one, but keep close to my young women. 9Let your eyes be on the field that they are reaping, and go after them. Have I not charged the young men not to touch you? And when you are thirsty, go to the vessels and drink what the young men have drawn." 10Then she fell on her face, bowing to the ground, and said to him, "Why have I found favor in your eyes, that you should take notice of me, since I am a foreigner?" 11But Boaz answered her, "All that you have done for your mother-in-law since the death of your husband has been fully told to me, and how you left your father and mother and your native land and came to a people that you did not know before. 12The LORD repay you for what you have done, and a full reward be given you by the LORD, the God of Israel, under whose wings you have come to take refuge!" 13Then she said, "I have found favor in your eyes, my lord, for you have comforted me and spoken kindly to your servant, though I am not one of your servants."

14And at mealtime Boaz said to her, "Come here and eat some bread and dip your morsel in the wine." So she sat beside the reapers, and he passed to her roasted grain. And she ate until she was satisfied, and she had some left over. 15When she rose to glean, Boaz instructed his young men, saying, "Let her glean even among the sheaves, and do not reproach her. 16And also pull out some from the bundles for her and leave it for her to glean, and do not rebuke her."

17So she gleaned in the field until evening. Then she beat out what she had gleaned, and it was about an ephah of barley. 18And she took it up and went into the city. Her mother-in-law saw what she had gleaned. She also brought out and gave her what food she had left over after being satisfied. 19And her mother-in-law said to her, "Where did you glean today? And where have you worked?

Blessed be the man who took notice of
you." So she told her mother-in-law with
whom she had worked and said, "The
man's name with whom I worked today is
Boaz." 20And Naomi said to her daughter-
in-law, "May he be blessed by the LORD,
whose kindness has not forsaken the
living or the dead!" Naomi also said to
her, "The man is a close relative of ours,
one of our redeemers." 21And Ruth the
Moabite said, "Besides, he said to me,
'You shall keep close by my young men
until they have finished all my harvest.'"
22And Naomi said to Ruth, her daughter-
in-law, "It is good, my daughter, that you
go out with his young women, lest in
another field you be assaulted." 23So she
kept close to the young women of Boaz,
gleaning until the end of the barley and
wheat harvests. And she lived with her
mother-in-law.

Go Deeper

Boaz was a kinsman redeemer for the family of Elimilech. The requirements he met to be such a redeemer are listed for you in this lesson. Because Boaz is an Old Testament type or picture of Jesus Christ, this "Go Deeper" compares those requirements with Christ's qualifications to be your personal Redeemer:

1. The redeemer must be a relative of the person redeemed. In Hebrews 2:11, Jesus calls us His brothers. So, without doubt, we are related to Him.

2. The person who would be the redeemer must be the closest kinsman possible to the one being redeemed. If the closest kinsman was unable or refused to redeem, the next in line could redeem. Romans 3:23 makes it clear, however, "all have sinned." That means there is no one else next in line who is able to redeem us, and everyone needs to be redeemed themselves—everyone but the sinless Jesus. Only He can redeem you.

3. The redeemer must be willing to pay the required price for redemption. Romans 6:23 tells us that the price necessary to pay for our sins is death. That's why Jesus, the One who gives life, submitted to death on the cross. He paid the price for you (1 Pet. 1:18–19).

4. The person who would be the redeemer must not be in debt himself. Jesus is the only one who is not stained with the debt of sin and, therefore, the only one who could redeem us (Heb. 4:15).

Jesus met all the requirements. He came to earth specifically to die for you so that He could be your redeemer and provide you with an abundant life (John 10:10). If you haven't thanked Him yet today for doing that, what are you waiting for?

In Ruth 2:1, we encounter Boaz for the first time. Ruth was looking for a way to provide food for herself and her mother-in-law. Since it was time to harvest barley, she decided she would glean in the fields rich with grain. Gleaning involved following the harvesters and picking up the grain that fell to the ground. (Jewish farmers were required by law not to reap the corners of the fields or to reap the fields bare. They were to allow some grain to remain for the benefit of foreigners and the poor. See Lev. 19:9.) It was hard, dirty work and, sometimes, unsafe for a woman. But one day—by the grace of God—Ruth found herself working in the field of a wealthy landowner named Boaz.

Think about what we know of Boaz. Ruth 2:1 describes him as a "worthy" man. Many versions translate the word "worthy" as "wealthy," but that word also carries the idea of "virtue" or "valor." So, Boaz wasn't simply a wealthy man; he was a man of principle.

He was also a man of faith. Verse 4 says, "And behold, Boaz came from Bethlehem. And he said to the reapers, 'The LORD be with you!' And they answered, 'The LORD bless you.'" The word "LORD" is probably in all capital letters in your Bible. That's because the word is *Jehovah* or *Yahweh*. It's the personal name of the God of Israel. Boaz believed in a living God whose presence was a reality in his life.

Boaz was also a man of integrity, an upright man, a caring man according to verses 8–16. In fact, Boaz is a wonderful type (illustration) of the love and grace the Lord Jesus has for His Church—you and me.

Look at verses 8–16 and specifically note four ways Boaz showed grace to Ruth. Compare that to the way God shows grace to you.

(1) Boaz instructed Ruth not to go to any other field to glean but to stay in his field. He didn't want to let her out of his watchful, loving care. He chose to begin a special relationship with her. That's exactly what the Lord Jesus does for us when we choose to follow Him. Psalm 91 paints a tender picture of how God cares for us: "He will cover you with his pinions, and under his wings you will find refuge" (v. 4). Not only does God care for us when we follow Christ, we also begin a special relationship with the Lord

> *"His willingness to serve as Kinsman-Redeemer for you and me goes far beyond requirements and qualifications to love. Christ loves us with an everlasting love, a sacrificial love, a love that He proved at a place called Calvary."*

Jesus that will last forever. We will never be out of His loving care (Deut. 31:6; Heb. 13:5).

(2) In Ruth 2:9, Boaz instructed the young men not to touch Ruth. Boaz was a man of integrity. He made sure Ruth would not be molested and no one would force her to leave. In the same way, God will protect you as well. John 10:27–29 says, "My sheep hear my voice, and I know them, and they follow me. I give them eternal life, and they will never perish, and no one will snatch them out of my hand. My Father, who has given them to me, is greater than all, and no one is able to snatch them out of the Father's hand." God loves you that much. Ruth enjoyed the promise of Boaz's protection; God gives you the same promise.

(3) Boaz showed grace to Ruth in 2:14 by inviting her to come and eat at his table. In that simple act, he confirmed the special relationship he'd begun with Ruth. Just as it is today, the table was a place for fellowship and community. Boaz extended the invitation and then bore the expense of everything at that table just as Christ bore the expense of everything we receive from Him. He gave His life for our salvation. It was grace that made Him do that.

(4) Boaz asked his young men to leave some grain on purpose for Ruth to glean (v. 16). This was above and beyond obedience to the Law; it was an intentional sacrifice on Boaz's part. It shows us what Christ did when He humbled Himself, left His home in heaven, and willingly died on a cross for us—so much more than we would ever expect God to do.

Look at Ruth's response to Boaz's grace in verses 10 and 13. Notice how amazed and unworthy Ruth felt. She can't believe that Boaz is treating her with such kindness. Think about a time when God's great goodness was clearly evident to you. In that moment, you probably felt exactly like Ruth did. Sometimes it can be a real challenge to comprehend God's love and grace or to realize how much His kindness has impacted our lives.

In verse 20 we learn a new piece of information about Boaz. Naomi, Ruth's mother-in-law, mentions that Boaz is a relative and "one of our redeemers." Boaz was a kinsman redeemer for the clan of Elimelech. In some cases, a kinsman redeemer would marry another man's widow and have children in the name of the dead man to carry on his line. In other circumstances, a poor Israelite who could not keep his family together could sell himself and his family. In that case, the kinsman redeemer might buy back the land and the family. In ancient Israel, this was a way to protect the clan by keeping the family and land of each tribe together. The Bible laid out strict guidelines for kinsman redeemers:

1. The redeemer must be a relative of the person redeemed (Lev. 25:47–49).
2. The person who would be the redeemer must be the closest kinsman possible to the one being redeemed. If the closest kinsman was unable or refused to redeem, the next in line could redeem (Ruth 3:12–13).
3. The redeemer must be willing to pay the required price for redemption (Lev. 25:50).
4. The person who would be the redeemer must not be in debt himself (or he'd be unable to buy back his kinsman or the land).

The "Go Deeper" section of our study shows how Christ meets all the criteria to be our Kinsman-Redeemer. But His willingness to serve as Kinsman-Redeemer for you and me goes far beyond requirements and qualifications to love. Christ loves us with an everlasting love, a sacrificial love, a love that He proved at a place called Calvary.

Express It

Remember the timeline you created in the first chapter, reviewing your life as a believer? Go back to it. Is there someone who has reflected Christ's love to you as Boaz did to Ruth? Thank God for placing that person in your life. Then, take a few moments to express your thanks. Give him or her a call; write a note or e-mail; and then say a special prayer for God's blessing in that person's life today.

Consider It

As you read Ruth 2, consider these questions:

1) What does Ruth's willingness to glean in the fields reveal about her?

____

____

2) What sorts of things had Boaz heard about Ruth?

____

____

3) What impressed Boaz's men about Ruth's work ethic?

____

____

4) Why did Ruth find it unusual that Boaz should take notice of her?

____

____

5) How did Ruth respond to the kindness Boaz showed her?

____

____

6) Besides the grain Ruth gleaned, what did she give Naomi when she returned home?

____

____

7) Did you notice a change in Naomi's attitude from chapter 1 to chapter 2?

____

____

8) Read Matthew 6:27–29. How does Ruth's experience in her new home relate to this passage?

____

____

Waiting Grace

How difficult is it for you when God asks you to wait? Next time you're called on to wait, take note of how you respond and make a conscious effort to trust God.

Ruth 3

Ruth and Boaz at the Threshing Floor

3 Then Naomi her mother-in-law said to her, "My daughter, should I not seek rest for you, that it may be well with you? [2]Is not Boaz our relative, with whose young women you were? See, he is winnowing barley tonight at the threshing floor. [3]Wash therefore and anoint yourself, and put on your cloak and go down to the threshing floor, but do not make yourself known to the man until he has finished eating and drinking. [4]But when he lies down, observe the place where he lies. Then go and uncover his feet and lie down, and he will tell you what to do." [5]And she replied, "All that you say I will do."

> ## Key Verse
>
> "*Wash therefore and anoint yourself, and put on your cloak and go down to the threshing floor, but do not make yourself known to the man until he has finished eating and drinking*" (Ruth 3:3).

[6]So she went down to the threshing floor and did just as her mother-in-law had commanded her. [7]And when Boaz had eaten and drunk, and his heart was merry, he went to lie down at the end of the heap of grain. Then she came softly and uncovered his feet and lay down. [8]At midnight the man was startled and turned over, and behold, a woman lay at his feet! [9]He said, "Who are you?" And she answered, "I am Ruth, your servant. Spread your wings over your servant, for you are a redeemer." [10]And he said, "May you be blessed by the Lord, my daughter. You have made this last kindness greater than the first in that you have not gone after young men, whether poor or rich. [11]And now, my daughter, do not fear. I will do for you all that you ask, for all my fellow townsmen know that you are a worthy woman. [12]And now it is true that I am a redeemer. Yet there is a redeemer nearer than I. [13]Remain tonight, and in the morning, if he will redeem you, good; let him do it. But if he is not willing to redeem you, then, as the Lord lives, I will redeem you. Lie down until the morning."

[14]So she lay at his feet until the morning, but arose before one could recognize another. And he said, "Let it not be known that the woman came to the threshing floor." [15]And he said, "Bring the garment you are wearing and hold it out." So she held it, and he measured out six measures of barley and put it on her. Then she went into the city. [16]And when she came to her mother-in-law, she said, "How did you fare, my daughter?" Then she told her all that the man had done for her, [17]saying, "These six measures of barley he gave to me, for he said to me, 'You must not go back empty-handed to your mother-in-law.'" [18]She replied, "Wait, my daughter, until you learn how the matter turns out, for the man will not rest but will settle the matter today."

Go Deeper

Naomi's last advice to Ruth in chapter 3 was to wait—"Wait, my daughter, until you learn how the matter turns out" (v. 18.) Waiting is sometimes the hardest part of dealing with difficult circumstances. It is human nature to want to do something. But often we rush in and do the wrong thing. It's important to take wise and informed steps when we face a dilemma. Often those steps are taken after much prayer for direction. The next time you face an unpleasant situation, take that difficulty to the Lord and ask His guidance rather than rushing in and trying to "fix things." He is a God of grace, and He will give you His grace when you need it most.

Here are some things you can be doing while you wait on God:

1. Be the person God wants you to be. Ruth remained the person God wanted her to be. She was loyal to Naomi; she remained pure; she kept living her life the right way—the godly way.

2. Do the things God wants you to do. Keep up your prayer life and take time to read His Word.

3. Don't force the issue. Allow God to work. God will open the right door at the right time.

4. Take the necessary steps to be in the right place, the place where God can work.

After you've done all that—trust Him. He is sovereign. Enjoy resting in His sovereignty.

At this time in Israel (the time of the judges), during the harvest season, many farmers were robbed of grain. So, workers would spend the night on the threshing room floor to protect their harvest. Boaz, as the landowner, spent the night on the floor himself. This fact led to some unusual advice from Naomi to Ruth.

Naomi advised Ruth to go to the threshing room floor when Boaz retired for the night and lie down at his feet. This doesn't mean that Ruth would be offering herself to Boaz sexually. Boaz's feet were to be the only part of his body uncovered. Ruth was a virtuous woman; Boaz was a virtuous man. Naomi could suggest this action to Ruth because she knew she could trust Boaz.

There is also a cultural meaning to the action Naomi suggested to Ruth. The Middle Eastern custom of lying down at the feet of a man

“You can leave everything in your life in God’s hands. He loves you. You can trust Him.”

and uncovering them was a culturally acceptable way for a woman to ask to be taken into a man’s family as his wife.

Going to Boaz in this way was also an act of humility. Ruth was telling him by her actions that she trusted him to do the right thing by her. Notice that Naomi assured Ruth that Boaz would tell her, when he discovered her at his feet, what to do next. This would communicate respect toward Boaz.

Ruth humbly followed her mother-in-law’s instructions. When Boaz woke during the night, he was startled to find a woman lying humbly at this feet. Ruth showed even greater humility by referring to herself as his “servant” (Ruth 3:9)—but she also bravely asked him to marry her with the words, “Spread your wings over your servant, for you are a redeemer” (v. 9). To this day, a Jewish man throws the end of his *talith* (prayer shawl) over his bride to demonstrate that he has taken her under his protection.

Ruth was within her rights to ask Boaz to marry her because she was the widow of Boaz’s relative, Mahlon. The law of levirate marriage, which required a man’s brother or a kinsman redeemer to marry his widow and preserve the family name, gave Ruth the right to expect such a marriage and the right to expect to have children who would carry on her dead husband’s name (Deut. 25:5). Ruth sought her rights, but she did so with humility.

Boaz’ next words (Ruth 3:10) tell us there was likely an age difference between Ruth and Boaz. Ruth, evidently, was drawn to Boaz because he was a man she could respect, a man who had values rather than someone she desired only because she was physically attracted to him. And it seemed to be mutual. As Ruth discovered she loved Boaz's character, Boaz admired Ruth's character qualities as well.

So, Boaz agreed to do as Ruth asked, but there was a conflict (every good romance has an element of conflict), a potential problem that could stop him from taking Ruth as his wife. There was another man who was a closer kinsman redeemer. In verse 13 Boaz instructed Ruth to lie down, assuring her that he would handle things in the morning.

Notice Boaz's words to Ruth, "If he [the closer redeemer] will redeem you, good; let him do it. But if he is not willing to redeem you, then, as the LORD lives, I will redeem you" (v. 13). Boaz left everything in God's hands. His words and subsequent actions reveal that he trusted God. He also verbalized a commitment both to God and to Ruth with those words. You, too, can leave everything in your life in God's hands. He loves you. You can trust Him.

Then in the closing scene of chapter 3, Ruth left the threshing floor before anyone was up for the day, and Boaz commanded his servants, "Let it not be known that the woman came to the threshing floor" (v. 14). His desire was to protect Ruth's reputation and also to protect the rights and interests of the closer kinsman redeemer. Before Ruth left, once again Boaz provided food for her and for her mother-in-law. Protection and provision—the very picture of our Lord and Savior.

Express It

In current culture, Ruth might have written a thank-you note in response to Boaz's kindness—a love letter if you will. Take some time to write your own love letter to God, thanking Him for His protection and provision in your life and admiring the qualities you see in Him. It doesn't have to be long; it just has to be sincere.

Consider It

As you read Ruth 3, consider these questions:

1) In what ways do you see God's provision for Ruth at the beginning of this chapter?

____

____

2) What reason did Naomi give Ruth for coming up with the plan to have Boaz redeem Ruth?

____

____

3) Why do you think Ruth followed Naomi's advice?

____

____

4) What six instructions did Naomi give Ruth?

____

____

5) What was Ruth's reputation around town?

____

____

6) According to Naomi, how quickly would Boaz resolve the matter of a closer redeemer?

____

____

7) How does Ruth demonstrate humility in this chapter?

____

____

8) Compare Ruth's words in verse 9, "Spread your wings over your servant, for you are a redeemer," with God's words to Israel in Ezekiel 16:8. How does God enter into a covenant with you by covering you with His garment? What does that mean to you?

____

____

Not without a Redeemer

Have there been times when you suddenly recognized that God was working out His plan in your life even though you hadn't seen any evidence until that moment? Was it easier for you to trust Him the next time you faced difficulty?

Ruth 4

Key Verse

"Blessed be the Lord *who has not left you this day without a redeemer"* (Ruth 4:14).

Boaz Redeems Ruth

4 Now Boaz had gone up to the gate and sat down there. And behold, the redeemer, of whom Boaz had spoken, came by. So Boaz said, "Turn aside, friend; sit down here." And he turned aside and sat down. 2And he took ten men of the elders of the city and said, "Sit down here." So they sat down. 3Then he said to the redeemer, "Naomi, who has come back from the country of Moab, is selling the parcel of land that belonged to our relative Elimelech. 4So I thought I would tell you of it and say, 'Buy it in the presence of those sitting here and in the presence of the elders of my people.'If you will redeem it, redeem it. But if you will not, tell me, that I may know, for there is no one besides you to redeem it, and I come after you." And he said, "I will redeem it." 5Then Boaz said, "The day you buy the field from the hand of Naomi, you also acquire Ruth the Moabite, the widow of the dead, in order to perpetuate the name of the dead in his inheritance." 6Then the redeemer said, "I cannot redeem it for myself, lest I impair my own inheritance. Take my right of redemption yourself, for I cannot redeem it."

7Now this was the custom in former times in Israel concerning redeeming and exchanging: to confirm a transaction, the one drew off his sandal and gave it to the other, and this was the manner of attesting in Israel. 8So when the redeemer said to Boaz, "Buy it for yourself," he drew off his sandal. 9Then Boaz said to the elders and all the people, "You are witnesses this day that I have bought from the hand of Naomi all that belonged to Elimelech and all that belonged to Chilion and to Mahlon. 10Also Ruth the Moabite, the widow of Mahlon, I have bought to be my wife, to perpetuate the name of the dead in his inheritance, that the name of the dead may not be cut off from among his brothers and from the gate of his native place. You are witnesses this day." 11Then all the people who were at the gate and the elders said, "We are witnesses. May the Lord make the woman, who is coming into your house, like Rachel and Leah, who together built up the house of Israel. May you act worthily in Ephrathah and be renowned in Bethlehem, 12and may your house be like the house of Perez, whom Tamar bore to Judah, because of the offspring that the Lord will give you by this young woman."

Ruth and Boaz Marry

13So Boaz took Ruth, and she became his wife. And he went in to her, and the Lord gave her conception, and she bore a son. 14Then the women said to Naomi, "Blessed be the Lord, who has not left you this day without a redeemer, and may his name be renowned in Israel! 15He shall be to you a restorer of life and a nourisher of your old age, for your daughter-in-law who loves you, who is more to you than seven sons, has given birth to him." 16Then Naomi took the child and laid him on her lap and became his nurse. 17And the women of the neighborhood gave him a name, saying, "A son has been born to Naomi." They named him Obed. He was the father of Jesse, the father of David.

The Genealogy of David

[18]Now these are the generations
of Perez: Perez fathered Hezron,
[19]Hezron fathered Ram, Ram fathered
Amminadab, [20]Amminadab fathered
Nahshon, Nahshon fathered Salmon,
[21]Salmon fathered Boaz, Boaz fathered
Obed, [22]Obed fathered Jesse, and Jesse
fathered David.

Go Deeper

Just as Boaz became Ruth's bridegroom, Jesus will become ours. Revelation 19:7–9 talks about the "marriage supper of the Lamb." What will we, the Bride, look like on that Day? The Bride of Christ will include people of all ages, all races, all economic brackets, all abilities and accomplishments who have believed in Christ as their Savior. Ephesians 5:27 tells us how we'll look: "without spot or wrinkle or any such thing, that she might be holy and without blemish." We are righteous because Christ's blood has washed us clean.

Comparing Christ to a bridegroom gives us some insight into the intimacy and the nearness to Him we will have in heaven. But even now, if you are a believer, you have His Spirit living in you—and you have only to go to His Word to experience His love expressed to you throughout the entire Scriptures. Look at verses like Galatians 2:20 that tell you, "Son of God, who loved me [you] and gave himself for me [you]," or John 15:9 where Jesus says, "As the Father has loved me, so have I loved you. Abide in my love," or the best-known verse in the Bible, John 3:16, "For God so loved the world, that he gave his only Son, that whoever believes in him should not perish but have eternal life."

His love for us is the reason for God's grace in our lives. Romans 5:2 says, "Through him we have also obtained access by faith into this grace in which we stand, and we rejoice in hope of the glory of God."

It's a marvelous truth that you will share in God's glory as the Bride of Christ!

Since we began this study of Ruth, we've seen much change in her life. She left her homeland in Moab and moved to Israel. She left her family and left her gods. The changes have been many, but they all proved to be God's grace to Ruth. Ruth was not a Hebrew, not one of the chosen people. She was a Gentile, a non-Jew. Yet, in His infinite wisdom and grace, God chose Ruth. He made Himself known to her and drew her to a saving faith in Him. Look at the direct ancestors of Christ, and you will see that Ruth is among them (Matt. 1:5). The God of Israel welcomes people of all nations—Hebrews and Gentiles alike. He can transform anyone.

In our study we have now come to Ruth 4. When we finished chapter 3, Ruth was heading home from the threshing room floor; in chapter 4, Boaz's first order of business was to talk to the closer kinsman redeemer (see chapter 2) to see whether or not the man wanted to redeem Mahlon's land and widow. You can read about Boaz's encounter with the closer kinsman redeemer in chapter 4:1–12. Notice the steps Boaz took to make sure he had witnesses to what was transpiring. And note the respect Boaz showed the other potential redeemer. He told the man the situation and allowed him to make his decision without any deception or coercion. This confidence demonstrates Boaz's respect for others and his faith in God's sovereignty in his life.

Finally in verse 13 we reach the moment we've been anticipating: Boaz and Ruth get married. There was a God-given conception too. Ruth had been barren in Moab. Now, her faithful obedience was rewarded by God. She had learned the truth that obedience to her God always brings reward.

Ruth's life wasn't the only one changed—so was Naomi's. The sad, bitter woman we saw in Ruth 1:20 has turned into a renewed and revitalized person. In fact, the town's women directed these amazing words to Naomi in Ruth 4:14–15: "Blessed be the Lord, who has not left you this day without a redeemer, and may his name be renowned in Israel! He shall be to you a restorer of life and a nourisher of your old age." Naomi had become a woman filled with joy and blessing. This little baby boy God sent into her life gave her a new purpose—she would be his nurse. Ruth and Boaz would care for Naomi the rest

"When you've gone through tough times—the loss of your husband or the loss of a child or a job loss—and you don't understand, remember that the blessing of God comes when we're faithful and obedient to Him. Our part is to wait and trust."

of her life. She could no longer say, "I went away full, and the Lord has brought me back empty" (1:21).

So, what caused this change? What made such a difference in the lives of these two women? The difference for both Ruth and Naomi was redemption—the kinsman redeemer changed their lives.

As we've said, in the story of Ruth, Boaz is a type or picture of Christ, who is our Kinsman-Redeemer. Because of sin, we are separated from God. But while we are alone and struggling to survive on our own, "while we were still sinners, Christ died for us" (Rom. 5:8). Jesus bought us back from sin just like Boaz bought the property and redeemed Ruth. He meets our needs, just as Boaz met Ruth's needs. As Boaz loved Ruth, Jesus loves us—He gave His life on Calvary's cross for us. He transforms us and our situation.

He works out the "conflicts" in our lives, just like Boaz handled the situation with the closer kinsman redeemer. Your conflict might be a confusing choice. He can guide you (Ps. 31:3). It might be a devastating loss. He can "bind up the broken-hearted" (Isa. 61:1). God is sovereign in your circumstances just like He was in Ruth's.

Christ is our Boaz, our Kinsman-Redeemer; when we trust Him as our Savior, He becomes our Bridegroom, and we, as the Church, become His Bride. In Ephesians 5:25–27, the apostle Paul compares the love of a husband to Christ's love for His Church. Then he instructs husbands to "love your wives, as Christ loved the church and gave himself up for her." And Revelation 19:7–9 talks about the "marriage of the Lamb," the union between Christ and His Church. Both passages refer to the righteousness of the Bride provided to us by Christ who washes us so that we are "without spot or wrinkle or any such thing, that she might be holy and without blemish" (Eph. 5:27).

Naomi is bouncing a baby on her knee in Ruth 4:16. What a joy that must have given a woman who returned to Judah empty. When you've gone through tough times—the loss of your husband or the loss of a child or a job loss—and you don't understand, remember that the blessing of God comes when we're faithful and obedient to Him. Our part is to wait and trust. Ruth and Naomi experienced the blessings of God because they waited on the Lord. They lived righteously before God. Faithfulness always brings reward.

The child, Ruth and Boaz's son, Obed, was an ancestor of the Lord Jesus. He brought blessings and joy to Ruth, Naomi, and Boaz. He brought new life to Naomi, a woman once weighed down by the bitterness of sorrow, and he was part of God's amazing plan to bring a Savior into the world for you and me.

We should expect to experience new life because of our Redeemer. In fact, Isaiah 42:9 says, "Behold, the former things have come to pass, and new things I now declare." Do you want "new things" in your life—ordered by Someone who loves you? Trust your Redeemer—Jesus Christ.

Express It

What does it mean to you that God has not left you without a redeemer but has sent Christ to set you free and provide eternal life for you? How would your life be different if you lived every day knowing that you had no access to God and no hope of heaven? Make a list of the things Christ provides for you as your Redeemer and thank Him for His abundant grace to you.

Consider It

As you read Ruth 4, consider these questions:

1) What character traits did Boaz demonstrate in his approach to the other kinsman redeemer?

2) How many men did Boaz have witness his transaction with the other kinsman redeemer?

3) What reason did the potential kinsman redeemer give for not redeeming Ruth and the land?

4) In verses 11–12, what four things did the elders include in their blessing for Ruth and Boaz?

5) The women in verse 14 give credit to God for Naomi's renewal. What has occurred in your life that you can give God credit for today?

6) In verse 15, what did the townswomen say that the baby would be to Naomi?

7) Who named Ruth and Boaz's baby?

Esther

The Silence of God

We should never think that God's silence is His absence. It isn't. In the account of Esther, God is not obviously present. He doesn't speak through either prophets or patriarchs. In fact, He's never directly mentioned or addressed in the Book of Esther, and His presence is only implied in a call for a time of fasting among His people.

But don't be discouraged or disturbed by this silence. He is still very much involved in the destinies of kings and in the lives of His people. Even when God is silent, His people need to be faithful and obedient to Him because He is not absent. You'll see that frequently in the lives of Esther and Mordecai.

Esther 1–2:18

> ## *Key Verse*
>
> *The king loved Esther more than all the women, and she won grace and favor in his sight more than all the virgins, so that he set the royal crown on her head and made her queen instead of Vashti* (Esther 2:17).

The King's Banquets

1 Now in the days of Ahasuerus, the
Ahasuerus who reigned from India to
Ethiopia over 127 provinces, [2]in those
days when King Ahasuerus sat on his
royal throne in Susa, the capital, [3]in the
third year of his reign he gave a feast for
all his officials and servants. The army
of Persia and Media and the nobles and
governors of the provinces were before
him, [4]while he showed the riches of
his royal glory and the splendor and
pomp of his greatness for many days,
180 days. [5]And when these days were
completed, the king gave for all the
people present in Susa, the citadel, both
great and small, a feast lasting for seven
days in the court of the garden of the
king's palace. [6]There were white cotton
curtains and violet hangings fastened
with cords of fine linen and purple to
silver rods and marble pillars, and also
couches of gold and silver on a mosaic
pavement of porphyry, marble, mother-
of-pearl and precious stones. [7]Drinks
were served in golden vessels, vessels of
different kinds, and the royal wine was
lavished according to the bounty of the
king. [8]And drinking was according to this
edict: "There is no compulsion." For the
king had given orders to all the staff of
his palace to do as each man desired.
[9]Queen Vashti also gave a feast for the
women in the palace that belonged to
King Ahasuerus.

Queen Vashti's Refusal

[10]On the seventh day, when the heart
of the king was merry with wine, he
commanded Mehuman, Biztha, Harbona,
Bigtha and Abagtha, Zethar and Carkas,
the seven eunuchs who served in the
presence of King Ahasuerus, [11]to bring
Queen Vashti before the king with her
royal crown, in order to show the peoples
and the princes her beauty, for she was
lovely to look at. [12]But Queen Vashti
refused to come at the king's command
delivered by the eunuchs. At this the
king became enraged, and his anger
burned within him.

[13]Then the king said to the wise men
who knew the times (for this was the
king's procedure toward all who were
versed in law and judgment, [14]the men
next to him being Carshena, Shethar,
Admatha, Tarshish, Meres, Marsena,
and Memucan, the seven princes of
Persia and Media, who saw the king's
face, and sat first in the kingdom):
[15]"According to the law, what is to be
done to Queen Vashti, because she has
not performed the command of King
Ahasuerus delivered by the eunuchs?"
[16]Then Memucan said in the presence
of the king and the officials, "Not only
against the king has Queen Vashti done
wrong, but also against all the officials
and all the peoples who are in all the
provinces of King Ahasuerus. [17]For the
queen's behavior will be made known to
all women, causing them to look at their
husbands with contempt, since they will
say, 'King Ahasuerus commanded Queen
Vashti to be brought before him, and
she did not come.' [18]This very day the

noble women of Persia and Media who
have heard of the queen's behavior will
say the same to all the king's officials,
and there will be contempt and wrath
in plenty. [19]If it please the king, let a
royal order go out from him, and let
it be written among the laws of the
Persians and the Medes so that it may
not be repealed, that Vashti is never
again to come before King Ahasuerus.
And let the king give her royal position
to another who is better than she. [20]So
when the decree made by the king is
proclaimed throughout all his kingdom,
for it is vast, all women will give honor
to their husbands, high and low alike."
[21]This advice pleased the king and the
princes, and the king did as Memucan
proposed. [22]He sent letters to all the
royal provinces, to every province in its
own script and to every people in its own
language, that every man be master in
his own household and speak according
to the language of his people.

Esther Chosen Queen

2 After these things, when the anger
of King Ahasuerus had abated, he
remembered Vashti and what she had
done and what had been decreed
against her. [2]Then the king's young men
who attended him said, "Let beautiful
young virgins be sought out for the king.
[3]And let the king appoint officers in all
the provinces of his kingdom to gather
all the beautiful young virgins to the
harem in Susa the capital, under custody
of Hegai, the king's eunuch, who is in
charge of the women. Let their cosmetics
be given them. [4]And let the young
woman who pleases the king be queen
instead of Vashti." This pleased the king,
and he did so.

[5]Now there was a Jew in Susa the
citadel whose name was Mordecai, the
son of Jair, son of Shimei, son of Kish,
a Benjaminite, [6]who had been carried
away from Jerusalem among the captives
carried away with Jeconiah king of Judah,
whom Nebuchadnezzar king of Babylon
had carried away. [7]He was bringing up
Hadassah, that is Esther, the daughter
of his uncle, for she had neither father
nor mother. The young woman had a
beautiful figure and was lovely to look
at, and when her father and her mother
died, Mordecai took her as his own
daughter. [8]So when the king's order and
his edict were proclaimed, and when
many young women were gathered in
Susa the citadel in custody of Hegai,
Esther also was taken into the king's
palace and put in custody of Hegai,
who had charge of the women. [9]And the
young woman pleased him and won his
favor. And he quickly provided her with
her cosmetics and her portion of food,
and with seven chosen young women
from the king's palace, and advanced
her and her young women to the best
place in the harem. [10]Esther had not
made known her people or kindred, for
Mordecai had commanded her not to
make it known. [11]And every day Mordecai
walked in front of the court of the harem
to learn how Esther was and what was
happening to her.

[12]Now when the turn came for each
young woman to go in to King Ahasuerus,
after being twelve months under the
regulations for the women, since this was
the regular period of their beautifying,
six months with oil of myrrh and six
months with spices and ointments for
women—[13]when the young woman went
in to the king in this way, she was given
whatever she desired to take with her
from the harem to the king's palace. [14]In
the evening she would go in, and in the
morning she would return to the second
harem in custody of Shaashgaz, the
king's eunuch, who was in charge of the
concubines. She would not go in to the
king again, unless the king delighted in
her and she was summoned by name.

[15]When the turn came for Esther
the daughter of Abihail the uncle of
Mordecai, who had taken her as his own

daughter, to go in to the king, she asked for nothing except what Hegai the king's eunuch, who had charge of the women, advised. Now Esther was winning favor in the eyes of all who saw her. [16]And when Esther was taken to King Ahasuerus, into his royal palace, in the tenth month, which is the month of Tebeth, in the seventh year of his reign, [17]the king loved Esther more than all the women, and she won grace and favor in his sight more than all the virgins, so that he set the royal crown on her head and made her queen instead of Vashti. [18]Then the king gave a great feast for all his officials and servants; it was Esther's feast. He also granted a remission of taxes to the provinces and gave gifts with royal generosity.

Go Deeper

Among other things, the Book of Esther is a valuable tool to give us historical insight into what was happening to the Jewish people as they were scattered throughout the ancient world. The events of the Book of Esther took place almost 500 years before the birth of Christ. This book records events that occurred about 100 years after the leading citizens of Israel were carried into Babylonian exile, about the year 587 B.C.

You may remember from reading the Book of Ezra or Nehemiah or even secular history that shortly after the Persians overthrew the Babylonians, they allowed many of the Jewish exiles to return to their native land. While a lot of them did, some chose to remain. Esther and her family were among those who chose to remain.

Esther was crowned queen in 478 B.C. This would have been during the height of the Persian Empire, when it consisted of nearly two million square miles of territory, spread from southern Egypt west to the Aegean, all the way to India (or Pakistan as we would call it today), from the Persian Gulf to the Black Sea and the Caspian Sea. An estimated 70 million people lived within its borders in the largest empire in the world up to that time. Ahasuerus was the king. Although he had a group of nobles close to the throne for advice, they had no share in governing, and he ruled with absolute power. He succeeded his father, King Darius I and regained Egypt for the Persian Empire but failed to conquer the Greeks. He was murdered in 464 B.C.

The Book of Esther focuses on those Jews who remained behind in the Persian Empire—those who did not go back to their homeland in Israel. It's the story of how God not only protected them, but provided for them in the midst of a powerful, foreign nation.

The Book of Esther, one of only two books in the Bible that tells the story of a woman, is unique in several ways. First, as mentioned already, God seems to be silent and out of sight. As you read, picture this story as a play on a grand stage. While you can't see or hear Him, God is both the author and director; He is even the stage manager, working ceaselessly behind the scenes to get the right people into the right place at just the right time.

Secondly, the story of Esther is set in Babylon, completely removed from Israel, the land God had chosen for His people. About 100 years have passed since the Israelites were carried into Babylon as exiles. There have also been a few changes on the world political scene. The Babylonian Empire was overthrown by the Persians who had allowed many of the Jewish exiles to return to their native land. While many did, thousands of Jews chose to remain behind. They had settled down there, raised a generation or two by now, and many had established businesses within this mighty empire. It had become their home.

A third distinction of Esther is that it takes place within the household of the Persian king, Xerxes. While he's referred to here as Ahasuerus, that name is more of a title than a personal name, just as *Caesar* was used later by the Romans. Ahasuerus ruled the vast Persian Empire which stretched from India to Egypt. He would have been the most powerful man in the world at this time and, as the Book of Esther opens, he has decided to show off his tremendous wealth and power with six months of grand feasting for all the princes, nobles, and important men of his empire.

That's when the trouble—and the story of Esther—begins.

While the king was feasting and showing off, his queen, Vashti, hosted her own festivities because it was not the custom for women to take part in feasting and frivolity with men in a Middle Eastern court. You can read the details in Esther 1:3–8. At the end of seven days, "when the heart of the king was merry with wine" (1:10), he commanded Vashti to come before them because he wanted to show off the beauty of his trophy wife. "But Queen Vashti refused to come at the king's command delivered by the eunuchs. At this the king became enraged, and his anger burned within him" (v. 12).

"Even when God is silent, you can still be certain that He is working in your life, and you must be faithful and obedient."

Vashti's insubordination in refusing to appear before the drunken king, however justified it may have been, meant serious trouble for him. His advisors and wise men were concerned as well that she would set a precedent for women throughout the empire. Their worry was that "this very day the noble women of Persia and Media who have heard of the queen's behavior will say the same to all the king's officials, and there will be contempt and wrath in plenty" (v. 18).

It was a significant concern, so the wise men came up with a plan for Ahasuerus. First, remove Vashti from her position as queen and banish her from the king's presence forever. Then select a replacement—a beautiful but (hopefully) more submissive woman to be queen. This advice greatly pleased the arrogant king, and he launched the world's first recorded beauty pageant.

Enter Esther. She was young and beautiful. She lived with Mordecai, an older cousin who had adopted her. Mordecai took Esther to the palace to be a contestant in the pageant. He was a wise and a devout Israelite. Mordecai probably taught Esther the glorious truths about God and the chosen people of Israel. Esther 2:7 says "the young woman had a beautiful figure and was lovely to look at" and she pleased and "won favor" with those she met (2:9,15,17).

This pageant took longer than the selection of an *American Idol* winner today. Each young woman was subjected to a beauty purification that lasted 12 months, a long-term spa treatment if you will. When presented to the king, she could use whatever she wanted to attract his attention. Esther went through the same process, with coaching from the eunuch in charge of the women, and one big secret: "Esther had not made known her people or kindred, for

Mordecai had commanded her not to make it known" (v. 10). Esther didn't tell the court that she was Jewish.

Esther 2:17 tells us how the pageant ended: "The king loved Esther more than all the women, and she won grace and favor in his sight more than all the virgins, so that he set the royal crown on her head and made her queen instead of Vashti."

Esther couldn't have understood or known why God was putting her in that position. The activities and attitudes of the Persian court would rarely have reflected the godly teaching Mordecai had given her. She was in a powerful but difficult position. Yet God sustained Esther, gave her favor in the eyes of the king, and positioned her in a place where He could use her life to accomplish His purposes.

It may have seemed that God was silent, but He was definitely involved, setting people and events in motion that would ensure the survival of His people. He had not forgotten those who were left behind in Babylon. In His providence, He moved Esther into the position of queen of the most powerful empire of the world at that time.

The Lord God still does that today. His silence is not the same as absence, and we must never see it that way. Even when He is silent, you can still be certain that He is working in your life, and you must be faithful and obedient. Keep your heart and mind open to His guidance. Trust Him each day, and one day you'll look back and understand everything just as He does now.

Express It

Recall a time when God sustained you in a confusing or troubling period in your life. Is there someone who might benefit today from your experience and the testimony God has given you? Tell someone about God's sustaining hand during the difficult time you remembered.

Consider It

As you read Esther 1–2:18, consider these questions:

1) Review the lavish banquet Ahasuerus hosts in Esther 1:5–8. As you consider the world around you, what similarities do you recognize?

2) Compare Ephesians 5:25 with Esther 1. How does Paul tell husbands to treat their wives?

3) Now compare Paul's instruction to wives in Ephesians 5:22 with Vashti's behavior toward Ahasuerus. How might Vashti have treated Ahasuerus in a more respectful manner?

4) What basis did the wise men use to justify their decision that Vashti should be banished?

5) Explain in your own words why Esther lives in the house of her cousin, Mordecai. Why do you think Esther kept her heritage a secret?

6) What does Esther 2:15 tell you about the character of this young woman?

7) How might remembering Esther's experience help you when God seems silent in your life?

Lesson 2

Conspiracy of Hatred

Throughout the centuries, followers of the One True God have been called to be set apart in mind, spirit, and action from the world around them. As you work through this study, consider how your actions set you apart from worldly values and behavior you see around you today.

Esther 2:19–3:15

Mordecai Discovers a Plot

19Now when the virgins were gathered
together the second time, Mordecai
was sitting at the king's gate. 20Esther
had not made known her kindred or her
people, as Mordecai had commanded
her, for Esther obeyed Mordecai just as
when she was brought up by him. 21In
those days, as Mordecai was sitting at
the king's gate, Bigthan and Teresh, two
of the king's eunuchs, who guarded the
threshold, became angry and sought to
lay hands on King Ahasuerus. 22And this
came to the knowledge of Mordecai, and
he told it to Queen Esther, and Esther
told the king in the name of Mordecai.
23When the affair was investigated and
found to be so, the men were both
hanged on the gallows. And it was
recorded in the book of the chronicles in
the presence of the king.

Key Verse

And when Haman saw that Mordecai did not bow down or pay homage to him, Haman was filled with fury. But he disdained to lay hands on Mordecai alone. So, as they had made known to him the people of Mordecai, Haman sought to destroy all the Jews, the people of Mordecai, throughout the whole kingdom of Ahasuerus (Esther 3:5–6).

Haman Plots Against the Jews

3 After these things King Ahasuerus
promoted Haman the Agagite, the
son of Hammedatha, and advanced
him and set his throne above all the
officials who were with him. 2And all the
king's servants who were at the king's
gate bowed down and paid homage to
Haman, for the king had so commanded
concerning him. But Mordecai did not
bow down or pay homage. 3Then the
king's servants who were at the king's
gate said to Mordecai, "Why do you
transgress the king's command?" 4And
when they spoke to him day after day
and he would not listen to them, they
told Haman, in order to see whether
Mordecai's words would stand, for he
had told them that he was a Jew. 5And
when Haman saw that Mordecai did not
bow down or pay homage to him, Haman
was filled with fury. 6But he disdained to
lay hands on Mordecai alone. So, as they
had made known to him the people
of Mordecai, Haman sought to destroy
all the Jews, the people of Mordecai,
throughout the whole kingdom of
Ahasuerus.

7In the first month, which is the month
of Nisan, in the twelfth year of King
Ahasuerus, they cast Pur (that is, they
cast lots) before Haman day after day;
and they cast it month after month till
the twelfth month, which is the month
of Adar. 8Then Haman said to King
Ahasuerus, "There is a certain people
scattered abroad and dispersed among
the peoples in all the provinces of your
kingdom. Their laws are different from
those of every other people, and they do
not keep the king's laws, so that it is not
to the king's profit to tolerate them. 9If
it please the king, let it be decreed that
they be destroyed, and I will pay 10,000
talents of silver into the hands of those
who have charge of the king's business,

that they may put it into the king's treasuries." [10]So the king took his signet ring from his hand and gave it to Haman the Agagite, the son of Hammedatha, the enemy of the Jews. [11]And the king said to Haman, "The money is given to you, the people also, to do with them as it seems good to you."

[12]Then the king's scribes were summoned on the thirteenth day of the first month, and an edict, according to all that Haman commanded, was written to the king's satraps and to the governors over all the provinces and to the officials of all the peoples, to every province in its own script and every people in its own language. It was written in the name of King Ahasuerus and sealed with the king's signet ring. [13]Letters were sent by couriers to all the king's provinces with instruction to destroy, to kill, and to annihilate all Jews, young and old, women and children, in one day, the thirteenth day of the twelfth month, which is the month of Adar, and to plunder their goods. [14]A copy of the document was to be issued as a decree in every province by proclamation to all the peoples to be ready for that day. [15]The couriers went out hurriedly by order of the king, and the decree was issued in Susa the citadel. And the king and Haman sat down to drink, but the city of Susa was thrown into confusion.

Go Deeper

Haman is clearly a serious enemy of the Jewish people living in Persia. We've already seen how he described them to Ahasuerus, but just how much does he hate the Jews? If "putting your money where your mouth is" is any way to judge, we can get a pretty good idea. "If it please the king, let it be decreed that they be destroyed, and I will pay 10,000 talents of silver into the hands of those who have charge of the king's business, that they may put it into the king's treasuries" (Esther 3:9). Talk about anti-Semitism! Haman is willing to pay 10,000 talents of silver, which is equivalent to about 750,000 pounds of silver. Do you realize what that would be worth today? A staggering sum. But he was willing to pay it because he hated the Jews so much.

The question is, Would the king accept it? He was a man of principle, but he had recently lost the battle of Salamis. His treasury was probably nearly empty. This offer of 10,000 talents of silver from Haman might be very attractive at this point. But Ahasuerus refused it. Josephus records that the king granted Haman's request, but he refused the money. Esther 3:11 says, "The money is given to you, the people also, to do with them as it seems good to you." Later Josephus, a Jewish historian (AD 37–c. 100), also noted that the king granted Haman's request but refused the money.

Within the royal court of a complex empire like Persia's, there would have been no shortage of intrigue and conspiracy. Rulers with absolute power are almost never popular, and if your empire includes conquered and assimilated peoples and cultures, long-standing prejudices don't disappear automatically.

In Esther 2:19–23, we catch a glimpse of this ugly reality. Mordecai, Esther's guardian, has taken up a place at the gates of the king's house. The Bible doesn't really explain why, but in ancient times the city gates were the gathering place for the wise men and elders to hear and judge matters of concern to the people. Perhaps, with Esther as queen, Mordecai was promoted to a new position too. Or maybe he was wise enough to stick close, keeping a watchful eye on Esther and serving as her eyes and ears to the world outside the palace.

Whatever the reason, Mordecai was in the right place at the right time to overhear an assassination plot on the king. He passed the information along to Esther, who in turn alerted the king, giving credit to Mordecai. The conspirators, Bigthan and Teresh, were summarily investigated, convicted and hung. King Ahasuerus lived to see another day. However, Mordecai received no reward, only a footnote in the detailed chronicles of the king. Don't forget that small detail. While the king seems to have a memory problem, God does not. When His people do the right thing, He will reward them. It may be a long time in coming, but He always rewards the faithfulness of His people. God keeps good records.

A second conspiracy appears in Esther 3, one that drives the rest of Esther's story. Things take an ugly turn with the introduction of the villain. In an old-fashioned melodrama, he would be dressed in black, have a cheesy moustache, and be greeted by boos and hisses from the audience. The Bible, however, keeps it simple and factual. "After these things King Ahasuerus promoted Haman the Agagite, the son of Hammedatha, and advanced him and set his throne above all the officials who were with him" (3:1).

“Obedience, integrity, and doing what’s right when compromise would be easier, often come at a great price.”

We know very little about Haman, and we’re given no real reason for this amazing promotion. He may have done the king a great service, contributed handsomely to the official treasury, or he may have been a favorite among the power-brokers of the day. It doesn’t matter. What does matter is that his new position carried with it power second only to the king and the right to be treated like royalty. It was probably much like the position Joseph gained in Egypt under Pharaoh. (See Gen. 41:37–57.)

According to Esther 3:2, “all the king’s servants who were at the king’s gate bowed down and paid homage to Haman, for the king had so commanded concerning him.” This is where the trouble begins. “But Mordecai did not bow down or pay homage.” The plot thickens.

Why the refusal? Why not just bow like everybody else? Well, in Esther 3:4, Mordecai explains that he is a Jew. While again we’re short on details, it’s clear that to bow to a man conflicted with what Mordecai believed was right. Bowing and giving homage would have been akin to worship. A righteous and faithful Jew like Mordecai would have remembered God’s command, “You shall have no other gods before me” (Ex. 20:3). Just like Shadrach, Meshach, and Abednego would not bow before Nebuchadnezzar’s idol in Daniel 3, Mordecai knew that obedience is always better than compromise. To offer near-worship to this puffed-up prime minister went against his conscience before God.

As a result of Mordecai’s insistence on obeying God, God’s people were put at risk. Obedience, integrity, and doing what’s right when compromise would be easier, often come at a great price.

When Haman heard of Mordecai's resistance, he was more than offended; he was "filled with fury" (Esther 3:5). In anger and injured pride, he was not satisfied "to lay hands on Mordecai alone" but "Haman sought to destroy all the Jews, the people of Mordecai, throughout the whole kingdom of Ahasuerus" (3:6). He rallied others to his plot and decided how to take care of the problem by the casting of lots or *Pur.* The Persians were a superstitious people who decided everyday things in their lives by casting lots, which meant throwing dice or drawing slips of wood or paper just as we might "draw straws" today. The lots determined the day (the 13th) and the month (Adar, the 12th month) that the Jews would be killed. If you're keeping track, that means that almost a year would pass before the Jews were to be exterminated.

Next Haman poured his poison in the king's ear and persuaded Ahasuerus that the Jews were a threat to his power and his treasury. Never mind that a Jew had just saved the king's life! No, "they do not keep the king's laws, so that it is not to the king's profit to tolerate them," Haman said (v. 8). Ahasuerus blindly bought the lies and issued a decree that the Jews, both young and old, men, women, and children, were to be annihilated.

Once the order was given and the news distributed, Haman and Ahasuerus sat down and enjoyed their wine (v. 15), but the people of the capital were "thrown into confusion," absolutely perplexed by what appeared to be a great injustice.

Two conspiracies: one against a king and the other against God's people. Does Haman's reaction seem extreme? One man made him angry, so he planned revenge on a whole race of people. But this hate-filled man failed to realize that the Lord preserves and protects those He calls His own. Whether by placing a righteous man like Mordecai at the king's gate or using the lots to give His people as much time as possible, God was silently at work. He doesn't forget those who obey Him. The plots and plans of man are still—and always will be—subject to the Lord's ultimate authority.

Today, there are many who hate God's people—both God's chosen people, the Jews, and His blood-bought people, those called by the name of Christ. In fact, the apostle John reminds us that we should "not be surprised, brothers, that the world hates you" (1 John 3:13). And Jesus told His followers—which includes us—that "in the world you will have tribulation. But take heart; I have overcome the world" (John 16:33).

No matter what conspiracies, prejudices, or outlandish difficulties you face today because of your faith, hold on to the hope God offers in His sovereign will. And take a page from Mordecai's book: Be faithful and obedient, even if the cost is high. God will not abandon you or forget you.

Express It

Is there someone in your life who has persecuted you, mistreated you, mocked your faith, or made themselves your enemy? Maybe this person is not your personal enemy, but would he or she be an enemy to the cause of Christ? Take some time to think about that person's needs and struggles. Ask God how you might pray for him or her. Then get down on your knees and offer a sincere prayer on this person's behalf. Challenging? Probably. In obedience to God's Word? Without a doubt!

Consider It

As you read Esther 2:19–3:15, consider these questions:

1) Like Ruth, Esther's life was full of changes. Compare and contrast the changes these women experienced and the situations they faced.

2) Esther 3:2 says Mordecai refused to kneel to Haman day after day. In what ways have you had to refuse "kneeling" before something that challenged God's rule in your life?

3) How could the events in Esther 2:19–3:15 be viewed as blessings from God?

4) When have you encountered a time where you had to remind yourself that God is in control?

5) Take a look at Esther 3:10 and note the title given to Haman. Now read Romans 12:14 and Matthew 5:44. How does God's Word instruct us to deal with our enemies?

6) How have you found it possible to follow the instructions God gives in Romans 12:14 and Matthew 5:44?

7) In Esther 3:1–15, what do you learn about the king's character?

For Such a Time as This

As believers, we are all called to serve God during our time on earth. Consider how this passage might apply to your work for Christ's kingdom and what Jesus is calling you to do in such a time as this.

Esther 4:1–17

Esther Agrees to Help the Jews

4 When Mordecai learned all that had
been done, Mordecai tore his clothes
and put on sackcloth and ashes, and
went out into the midst of the city, and
he cried out with a loud and bitter cry.
2He went up to the entrance of the king's
gate, for no one was allowed to enter the
king's gate clothed in sackcloth. 3And
in every province, wherever the king's
command and his decree reached, there
was great mourning among the Jews,
with fasting and weeping and lamenting,
and many of them lay in sackcloth and
ashes.

4When Esther's young women and
her eunuchs came and told her, the
queen was deeply distressed. She sent
garments to clothe Mordecai, so that
he might take off his sackcloth, but he
would not accept them. 5Then Esther
called for Hathach, one of the king's
eunuchs, who had been appointed to
attend her, and ordered him to go to
Mordecai to learn what this was and why
it was. 6Hathach went out to Mordecai in
the open square of the city in front of the
king's gate, 7and Mordecai told him all
that had happened to him, and the exact
sum of money that Haman had promised
to pay into the king's treasuries for the
destruction of the Jews. 8Mordecai also
gave him a copy of the written decree
issued in Susa for their destruction, that
he might show it to Esther and explain
it to her and command her to go to the
king to beg his favor and plead with him
on behalf of her people. 9And Hathach
went and told Esther what Mordecai had
said. 10Then Esther spoke to Hathach
and commanded him to go to Mordecai
and say, 11"All the king's servants and
the people of the king's provinces know
that if any man or woman goes to the
king inside the inner court without being
called, there is but one law—to be put to
death, except the one to whom the king
holds out the golden scepter so that he
may live. But as for me, I have not been
called to come in to the king these thirty
days."

Key Verse

"For if you keep silent at this time, relief and deliverance will rise for the Jews from another place, but you and your father's house will perish. And who knows whether you have not come to the kingdom for such a time as this?" (Esther 4:14).

12And they told Mordecai what Esther
had said. 13Then Mordecai told them to
reply to Esther, "Do not think to yourself
that in the king's palace you will escape
any more than all the other Jews. 14For
if you keep silent at this time, relief
and deliverance will rise for the Jews
from another place, but you and your
father's house will perish. And who
knows whether you have not come to the
kingdom for such a time as this?" 15Then
Esther told them to reply to Mordecai,
16"Go, gather all the Jews to be found
in Susa, and hold a fast on my behalf,
and do not eat or drink for three days,
night or day. I and my young women will
also fast as you do. Then I will go to the
king, though it is against the law, and if
I perish, I perish." 17Mordecai then went
away and did everything as Esther had
ordered him.

Go Deeper

We don't know much about Esther's personal faith in God. But we can see evidences of her faith in her actions. In verse 16, Esther requested a fast. Fasting is clearly biblical. Nineteen people are recorded to have fasted in the Bible in addition to 17 examples of corporate fasting. But it is very important that we fast for the right reasons. If we want to honor God with our fasting and allow our fasting to be useful for His purposes, we've got to read the Bible. We ought to learn all that the Bible has to say about fasting.

Secondly, we should make sure we don't look for unrealistic responses to our fasting. God will move when God chooses to move. Just because we add fasting to prayer doesn't mean we're going to speed up God or that He is required to act according to our plan.

The following additional scriptures refer to fasting:

Exodus 34:28; 1 Samuel 7:6, 31:11–13;
2 Samuel 1:12, 12:15–23;
2 Chronicles 20:3–4; Ezra 8:21–23;
Nehemiah 9:1–3; Psalm 35:13, 69:10;
Isaiah 58:5–7, 9–12; Jeremiah 36:6;
Daniel 10:2–3; Joel 1:14, 2:12;
Jonah 3:4–9; Zechariah 7:5–6;
Matthew 4:1–2, 6:16–18, 9:15;
Mark 2:19–20; Luke 4:1–2;
Acts 13: 2–3, 14:23.

Real heroes generally don't go looking for opportunities to save the world. They're often people who, at a given time, find it necessary to step up and do what needs to be done: the firefighter who goes back into a burning building for a child; the father who tackles a terrorist on his plane; or the woman who donates a kidney to her daughter. These are people who see the need, have the opportunity, and take action.

Esther was like that, a young woman in a unique position to take action and save her people. This chapter records the heart of courage and the story of a heroine which draws us back to the Book of Esther again and again.

Remember the end of Esther 3—A hate-driven Haman persuaded King Ahasuerus to issue an extermination order against the Jews (but with an extensive timeframe). The order included Mordecai, whose refusal to bow before Haman fueled his anger. But it would also include Esther, the queen with her secret identity—neither Haman nor the king knew she was a Jew.

"The Lord is in control of our lives. From the moment we're born to the day we die, our days are His. When we follow Him, we participate in His plans. God has placed each of us in His kingdom 'for such a time as this.'"

Chapter 4 opens with Mordecai's reaction to the royal edict. "When Mordecai learned all that had been done, Mordecai tore his clothes and put on sackcloth and ashes, and went out into the midst of the city, and he cried out with a loud and bitter cry" (v. 1). Sackcloth and ashes were traditional signs of extreme grief and distress. Mordecai took this symbolic step and the rest of the Jews spontaneously did exactly the same. Each put on the clothes of grief, weeping and wailing because it seemed certain they would all die.

Mordecai, in his mournful condition, went to the king's gate as usual but did not seek entrance. Due to palace protocol, no one was allowed to pass through the outer gate of the palace wearing sackcloth and ashes. This was when Esther first discovered there was a problem. She sent Mordecai fresh clothing, but when he rejected them, she sent her personal assistant to get the whole story.

As queen, Esther would have had little contact with the outside world. Her daily routine was taken up within the court, sequestered with the women and isolated from the king unless invited—no Internet, no *Persian News Network*, only what servants and messengers with access to the outside world could deliver. This made Mordecai's position at the king's gate so crucial. He was her eyes and ears; and evidently Hathach, a eunuch serving Esther, was one of the few she trusted with Mordecai's news and her secrets. As you read chapter 4, notice there is no direct conversation between Esther and Mordecai, only messages relayed through Hathach.

What's the message? Look again at Esther 4:6–8.

Did you notice Mordecai's goal here? He encouraged, even commanded, Esther to plead their case to the king. She was in a unique position of influence, but there's a hitch: You could only enter the king's presence by royal invitation. Everyone knows, Esther replied, that "if any man or woman goes to the king inside the inner court without being called, there is but one law—to be put to death, except the one to whom the king holds out the golden scepter so that he may live" (v. 11). She hadn't been invited for 30 days. So, Mordecai's request was very risky—but so was a lack of action. Either way, he reminded Esther in verses 13 and 14, she faced death. Her royal position would not be enough to save her from Haman's vengeful edict.

This is the moment every hero faces: the choice to put yourself on the line, to step up and take the risk or retreat and do nothing. Mordecai challenged Esther in verse 14: "For if you keep silent at this time, relief and deliverance will rise for the Jews from another place, but you and your father's house will perish. And who knows whether you have not come to the kingdom for such a time as this?"

Do you see the faith revealed in Mordecai's statement? He recognized that if Esther didn't rise to the occasion, God would bring relief and deliverance from somewhere. He held onto that hope, reminding us that God is our only hope even today. The other part of his statement acknowledged that Esther had an opportunity to be a part of God's plan. She just needed to be courageous and to take the risk as a willing participant with God.

The Lord is in control of our lives. From the moment we're born to the day we die, our days are His. When we follow Him, we participate in His plans. God has placed each of us in His kingdom "for such a time as this." You may become a world-changer, like Esther whose courage preserved God's people. Or you may be a life-changer, touching one person at just the right moment.

Esther's response to Mordecai was simple: "Go, gather all the Jews to be found in Susa, and hold a fast on my behalf, and do not eat or drink for three days, night or day. I and my young women will also fast as you do. Then I will go to the king, though it is against the law, and if I perish, I perish" (v. 16). The stakes are high; the situation is demanding; but the response is sure. Take the risk. Have courage. Be a hero.

Express It

Who knows whether you're here for such a time as this? To comfort a grieving friend, to offer hope to a hopeless young person, to be a listening ear and a tender touch to a hurting neighbor, to speak up against injustice at work, to be a voice for the voiceless in a nursing home, to provide for a needy stranger or point a seeking heart in God's direction. Make a short list of opportunities that exist for you to live out your faith. Then, follow Esther's lead and say, "Yes, Lord, whatever the cost."

Consider It

As you read Esther 4:1–17, consider these questions:

1) What do Mordecai's actions in verse 1 communicate to those around him? What do they communicate to Esther? To God?

2) Consider verse 4. Mordecai refused to accept the clean clothes from Esther. Why do you think he refused them? Do you find that your first instinct is usually to cover up a problem or to offer a quick but shallow fix? Why is that?

3) Esther had a trusted advisor in Mordecai and a trusted messenger in Hathach. Who do you turn to when you're in need of a trustworthy friend?

4) What was Esther's response when Hatach first told her about the decree for the Jew's death? What concern did she send back to Mordecai?

5) Write about a time when you were challenged to do something bold for God.

6) What opportunities in your life require you to step up and be the person God has placed there for just the specific occasion?

7) What can you do to ensure that you are depending on God during challenging circumstances?

Dress Rehearsal

Esther 5 is filled with preparations. As you read, think about how you prepare yourself for decisions, major events, or serving the Lord. Consider what you might do to glorify God in the process of your preparation.

Esther 5:1–14

Esther Prepares a Banquet

5 On the third day Esther put on her royal robes and stood in the inner court of the king's palace, in front of the king's quarters, while the king was sitting on his royal throne inside the throne room opposite the entrance to the palace. 2And when the king saw Queen Esther standing in the court, she won favor in his sight, and he held out to Esther the golden scepter that was in his hand. Then Esther approached and touched the tip of the scepter. 3And the king said to her, "What is it, Queen Esther? What is your request? It shall be given you, even to the half of my kingdom." 4And Esther said, "If it please the king, let the king and Haman come today to a feast that I have prepared for the king." 5Then the king said, "Bring Haman quickly, so that we may do as Esther has asked." So the king and Haman came to the feast that Esther had prepared. 6And as they were drinking wine after the feast, the king said to Esther, "What is your wish? It shall be granted you. And what is your request? Even to the half of my kingdom, it shall be fulfilled." 7Then Esther answered, "My wish and my request is: 8If I have found favor in the sight of the king, and if it please the king to grant my wish and fulfill my request, let the king and Haman come to the feast that I will prepare for them, and tomorrow I will do as the king has said."

Haman Plans to Hang Mordecai

9And Haman went out that day joyful and glad of heart. But when Haman saw Mordecai in the king's gate, that he neither rose nor trembled before him, he was filled with wrath against Mordecai. 10Nevertheless, Haman restrained himself and went home, and he sent and brought his friends and his wife Zeresh. 11And Haman recounted to them the splendor of his riches, the number of his sons, all the promotions with which the king had honored him, and how he had advanced him above the officials and the servants of the king. 12Then Haman said, "Even Queen Esther let no one but me come with the king to the feast she prepared. And tomorrow also I am invited by her together with the king. 13Yet all this is worth nothing to me, so long as I see Mordecai the Jew sitting at the king's gate." 14Then his wife Zeresh and all his friends said to him, "Let a gallows fifty cubits high be made, and in the morning tell the king to have Mordecai hanged upon it. Then go joyfully with the king to the feast." This idea pleased Haman, and he had the gallows made.

Key Verse

Then Esther answered, "My wish and my request is: If I have found favor in the sight of the king, and if it please the king to grant my wish and fulfill my request, let the king and Haman come to the feast that I will prepare for them, and tomorrow I will do as the king has said" (Esther 5:7–8).

Go Deeper

If you look back through the history of the Bible, God has constantly been bringing people to the right place at just the right time, people who would have the humility, wisdom, and courage to do His will. Abraham was a man who was called by God to live a life of faith in his day when no one else was. Noah was a man who found grace in the eyes of the Lord because of his righteous life. What about Moses? He is a man who spent 40 years on the back side of the desert, but when the time came, he stood up and took his place. King Saul was Satan's man. He was plunging the nation of Israel into sin and idolatry. But while all that was happening, God was training a young shepherd boy named David to become king "for such a time as this."

And what about John the Baptist? God had called him to be a voice "crying [for God] in the wilderness" (Matt. 3:3) after a silence of 400 years. John clearly was a man called to the kingdom for such a time as this. Saul of Tarsus, a brilliant rabbi, hated the Church, hated Christians, hated Christ. But all the time he was hating, God was preparing him to be an apostle to the Gentiles and one of the formulative minds of the early Christian Church.

All these people have one thing in common. They are all dead. They've had their day. Their day has come and gone. God raised them up for just the right time, but this is our day. This is your time and mine. God has raised us up for this generation. Are you willing to do what God wants you to do in this "your time"?

Have you ever watched the final rehearsals of a play? There's so much activity on and off stage as everyone works to get all the details just right. It may be the actors who tell the story on stage, but there's just as much drama going on backstage.

Consider the events of Esther 5 as one of those rehearsals. In 5:1–8, the big scene is rehearsed, but it's not quite "opening night." That's coming up in chapter 7. Then 5:9–14 offers the drama offstage as one of the players gets ready for his big moment.

On stage, Esther knows how to make an entrance! After three days of fasting and preparation, she's ready to face the king. This was not the time to drop in and say, "Hi, honey, how about a little lunch?" No, she turns up in her full royal regalia, almost like her coronation. She was determined to arrive in state and, if the king was displeased

"For a proud, ambitious man like Haman, this must have proved that he had arrived in the royal court. The world was his oyster; nothing could tarnish his glory."

with her unexpected visit, she would die in state too. Verse 1 is very specific about how Esther stood in front of the king. It is so specific that we cannot possibly think Esther approached the situation casually. Can you get a visual picture of Esther standing in the inner court, in front of the king's quarters, while the king is inside the throne room opposite the entrance? This was Esther's big moment, and her neck was on the line. Remember her resolve in Esther 4:16, "if I perish, I perish." She could face death by inaction or step up with courage. Clearly, she knew the risk.

Here Esther offers valuable insight into courage and obedience. When God calls us to step up, when He gives us an opportunity to speak out or be a hero, we need to be willing and prepared. Esther spent three days fasting and preparing for this day. Yes, at times we should act quickly to obey; but there is also great wisdom in taking time to prepare ourselves, listen to God, and familiarize ourselves with His will.

As chapter 5 proceeds, Esther made it into the king's presence—and out—alive. Her unexpected arrival actually pleased the king; he extended his royal scepter, and Esther touched the top of it in acceptance. Ahasuerus generously offered her whatever she wanted, even half the kingdom. Esther humbly extended to him the invitation to a private lunch for the king and his right-hand man, Haman. It was already prepared just as Esther herself was prepared. Remember, this was not your usual marriage or family. It was common in the ancient

Near East for the king and queen to dine separately, each in their own apartments with their own friends and attendants. It was not common for the queen to ask the king to come to lunch or to include another male guest who was not her relative. She invited Haman, too, and he was absolutely thrilled with this privileged opportunity.

The king accepted, and since this was such an unusual occurrence, the king evidently suspected there was something more going on. He raised the question again over lunch, but Esther only extended a second invitation for dinner the next evening.

Why the stall tactics? The Bible isn't clear. Perhaps there was an element of fear on Esther's part as she waited for the right moment or tried to find the right words. Perhaps Esther was wise enough to build the king's interest and make sure he was paying attention when she had something significant to say. By including Haman, she had a chance to see the enemy, to gauge his relationship with Ahasuerus and to avoid a situation that could become Haman's word against hers. Whatever Esther's reasons, it worked. The king was intrigued enough to accept the second invitation, and Haman's inflated pride was flattered and unsuspicious.

That's the dress rehearsal on stage. Opening night is just around the corner—but we also need to look behind the scenes.

Chapter 5:9–14 takes us backstage with Haman. He left the palace "joyful and glad of heart" (v. 9), but it doesn't last. "But when Haman saw Mordecai in the king's gate, that he neither rose nor trembled before him, he was filled with wrath against Mordecai" (v. 9). Just a few minutes earlier this man was flattered by the attention of the queen; now he's angry because Mordecai continues to ignore him.

However, Haman was not one to miss an opportunity for self-glorification. He regaled his wife and friends with the glory of his riches and boasted of all his great achievements. To cap it off, Haman proudly announced in verse 12, "'Even Queen Esther let no one but me come with the king to the feast she prepared. And tomorrow also I am invited by her together with the king.'" For a proud, ambitious man like Haman, this must have proved that he had arrived in the royal court. The world was his oyster; nothing could tarnish his glory.

Nothing? "Yet all this is worth nothing to me, so long as I see Mordecai the Jew sitting at the king's gate" (v. 13). Like a spoiled child, Haman was dissatisfied with all he had because Mordecai wouldn't give him the respect he thought he was due. There's never enough for those who live by their pride. It took the soothing promise of Mordecai's execution to cheer up Haman, and he was quick to set up the gallows. Only the promises of Mordecai's death would please him.

Esther 5 presents two contrasting people. One is Esther who acts in wisdom and proceeds with humility. We see that in her careful preparations and how she handles herself before the king. The other is Haman, lost in the folly of pride which colors his every action and drives him to hatred and vengeance. All his wealth and privileges could not buy him happiness; he was a captive to his own puffed-up ego and, as he's about to discover, the greater the pride, the more painful the humiliation. Haman needed to know what Esther probably understood, that "God opposes the proud, but gives grace to the humble" (James 4:6).

Express It

Did you know it's OK to tremble when you're doing God's work? What is not OK is to refuse to act when God has brought you "to the kingdom for such a time as this." If you are in a place right now where God is asking you to do something that has you a little fearful, resolve today to go forward in obedience. Spend some time alone with God asking Him to equip and encourage you.

Consider It

As you read Esther 5:1–14, consider these questions:

1) What character traits does Esther exhibit in verses 1–8?

2) In what ways could you display similar characteristics in a situation you presently face?

3) Why do you suppose Esther did not present her request to the king during this first meal together?

4) Make a list of the wise actions Esther took in this chapter.

5) Have you ever faced a situation where, like Esther, you were a little afraid and didn't quite know what to do in the midst of serving God?

6) Examine verse 9. What is it about Mordecai that fills Haman with such rage?

7) Now, examine your own heart. Have you ever been angered by someone because they injured your pride? How did you react?

8) Haman received advice from his friends and family that served only to inflate his pride. Sadly, he followed that advice. What can you do to make sure that you don't follow unwise advice?

The Bitter Price of Pride

Timing: it's crucial, isn't it? So often we would like to control the timing of events in our lives, but it seems out of our hands. In Esther 6, we see God's impeccable timing turn a dire situation into a glorious reward. So, what is it in your life that needs God's timing? Remember, God's timing may not be your timing, but it will be perfect!

Esther 6:1–13

The King Honors Mordecai

6 On that night the king could not sleep.
And he gave orders to bring the book of
memorable deeds, the chronicles, and
they were read before the king. 2And it
was found written how Mordecai had
told about Bigthana and Teresh, two of
the king's eunuchs, who guarded the
threshold, and who had sought to lay
hands on King Ahasuerus. 3And the king
said, "What honor or distinction has
been bestowed on Mordecai for this?"
The king's young men who attended him
said, "Nothing has been done for him."
4And the king said, "Who is in the court?"
Now Haman had just entered the outer
court of the king's palace to speak to
the king about having Mordecai hanged
on the gallows that he had prepared for
him. 5And the king's young men told him,
"Haman is there, standing in the court."
And the king said, "Let him come in."
6So Haman came in, and the king said
to him, "What should be done to the
man whom the king delights to honor?"
And Haman said to himself, "Whom
would the king delight to honor more
than me?" 7And Haman said to the king,
"For the man whom the king delights
to honor, 8let royal robes be brought,
which the king has worn, and the horse
that the king has ridden, and on whose
head a royal crown is set. 9And let the
robes and the horse be handed over to
one of the king's most noble officials.
Let them dress the man whom the king
delights to honor, and let them lead him
on the horse through the square of the
city, proclaiming before him: 'Thus shall
it be done to the man whom the king
delights to honor.'" 10Then the king said
to Haman, "Hurry; take the robes and
the horse, as you have said, and do so to
Mordecai the Jew, who sits at the king's
gate. Leave out nothing that you have
mentioned." 11So Haman took the robes
and the horse, and he dressed Mordecai
and led him through the square of the
city, proclaiming before him, "Thus shall
it be done to the man whom the king
delights to honor."

12Then Mordecai returned to the king's
gate. But Haman hurried to his house,
mourning and with his head covered.
13And Haman told his wife Zeresh and all
his friends everything that had happened
to him. Then his wise men and his wife
Zeresh said to him, "If Mordecai, before
whom you have begun to fall, is of the
Jewish people, you will not overcome him
but will surely fall before him."

Key Verse

Then the king said to Haman, "Hurry; take the robes and the horse, as you have said, and do so to Mordecai the Jew, who sits at the king's gate. Leave out nothing that you have mentioned" (Esther 6:10).

Go Deeper

An important point in this passage is that Mordecai had not sought any kind of reward for his good deed. Initially, he was passed over. Yet eventually, his actions were discovered and rewarded. Mordecai's humility stands in stark contrast to the pride of Haman. This contrast between pride and humility is found throughout Scripture. Take a look at Jesus' words about the effects of humility versus pride.

"But when you are invited, go and sit in the lowest place, so that when your host comes he may say to you, 'Friend, move up higher.' Then you will be honored in the presence of all who sit at table with you. For everyone who exalts himself will be humbled, and he who humbles himself will be exalted" (Luke 14:10–11).

God promises to exalt the humble but humble the proud. It's very tempting to announce our good deeds to those around us to make sure others know we are worthy of praise or have been given a high position. When you've done right and not been recognized for it, it can be especially difficult. But when we remember the character of our God, we know He never forgets and we can wait on His perfect timing for our reward. Even if you have to wait, wouldn't you rather have the rewards God offers which will make a prince like Ahasuerus look like a pauper? When God exalts, it is for good.

Do you enjoy a little irony? A sense of justice when someone gets a taste of what they deserve? It's OK; you can be honest. Many of us secretly like to see a proud or self-important person experience a touch of humility. It's poetic justice.

When reading Esther 6, we might be forgiven for thinking God smiled, at least a little, over popping Haman's bubble of pride. Unfortunately, pride is a problem we all share. Even in gloating over another's downfall, we become puffed up because we weren't the ones to fall. So, while you may enjoy a secret glee over Haman's humiliation, remember it could happen to you.

What burst Haman's bubble? Go back to Esther 3 and see how his pride has grown. He was promoted to second-in-command to King Ahasuerus, enjoying the good graces of the king, and he scored a private dinner engagement with the king and queen. The only thorn in his side was Mordecai, who sat at the palace and refused to bow

"God's sovereign but silent hand again intervened. The king just happened to be awake; he just happened to choose the historical records for his reading; and the section read just happened to include the time Mordecai uncovered an assassination plot against the king!"

before him. Haman found a solution to that problem, too, first by securing a royal decree to eliminate the Jews; and second, by building a gallows on which to hang Mordecai. Haman was so full of himself, he couldn't see much else going on.

However, there was a lot going on. God was silently engineering His plan, and His timing was impeccable, even in the details. He was protecting and honoring those who honored Him. While Haman was oblivious, God had missed nothing.

As Esther 6 opens, the king was having trouble sleeping. Earlier that day, Esther unexpectedly turned up to invite Haman and King Ahasuerus to lunch. After lunch, she invited them to a dinner planned for the following evening. Haman went off to gloat over his good fortune and then ordered the gallows for Mordecai. The king was on his own, but he couldn't sleep. Being a man of some pride and achievement, he chose a little light reading from the chronicles of his kingdom. Nothing soothes a sleepless king like the glorious details of his own accomplishments.

God's sovereign but silent hand again intervened. The king just happened to be awake; he just happened to choose the historical records for his reading; and the section read just happened to include the time Mordecai uncovered an assassination plot against the king! It was a few years back (Esther 2:19–23), but Ahasuerus discovered that Mordecai was never rewarded and he now wanted to correct that oversight. The librarians who selected the text to read to the king could have chosen any number of passages to read. In a book that contained 12 years of accounts, the men who read to King Ahasuerus selected the account of Mordecai uncovering an assassination plot. That is the sovereignty of God at work.

Timing is everything. The king needed advice, and the only person available was Haman. "Now Haman had just entered the outer court of the king's palace to speak to the king about having Mordecai hanged on the gallows that he had prepared for him" (6:4). Why did Haman come? To get the king's permission to hang Mordecai. Evidently Haman couldn't wait until the date set in the edict for destroying the Jews; he wanted revenge immediately. So, while he came for permission to hang Mordecai, Ahasuerus was looking for a way to reward Mordecai. Haman wanted one thing; the king wanted another. But God would have His way.

"So Haman came in, and the king said to him, 'What should be done to the man whom the king delights to honor?' And Haman said to himself, 'Whom would the king delight to honor more than me?'" (v. 6). Haman jumped to the logical conclusion of a proud mind. We all know people like that; and, if we're honest, at times we've been just like that ourselves.

So, Haman concocted an elaborate scheme to honor himself. "And Haman said to the king, 'For the man whom the king delights to honor, let royal robes be brought, which the king has worn, and the horse that the king has ridden, and on whose head a royal crown is set. And let the robes and the horse be handed over to one of the king's most noble officials. Let them dress the man whom the king delights to honor, and let them lead him on the horse through the square of the city, proclaiming before him: 'Thus shall it be done to the man whom the king delights to honor'" (vv. 7–9).

Imagine the look on Haman's face when the king told him to "do so to Mordecai the Jew, who sits at the king's gate'" (v. 10)! Surprise, horror, anger, shock, humiliation—within a split second his dreams were shattered. Not only would he miss the adulation he so craved, but he had to publicly honor his enemy, Mordecai. It was more than Haman could stand. In fact, when the parade was over, he returned home "mourning and with his head covered" (v. 12). This humiliation was like grieving a death, the death of his happy bubble of self-pride.

James 4:6 reminds us that "God opposes the proud, but gives grace to the humble," and Esther 6 illustrates that so well. While these events could be tossed aside as coincidence, look once again at the evidence that God was working to bring down a proud man and shower His grace on His humble servant: There was the 24-hour delay on Esther's banquet plans; the king was unable to sleep; the librarians' choice of reading material; Haman's early arrival; even the way the king asked the question about honoring a man. Every detail was engineered and used by God to bring honor to Mordecai and to teach Haman a thing or two about pride.

Pride is our great human struggle. It puffs us up to believe we're better than another person, that we deserve more, or that we can do our own thing in our own way because we know better. The greatest hazard of pride is that it leaves God out of the equation; it causes us to refuse to live in humble dependence on Him. Our pride may not be as obvious as Haman's, but it still carries a bitter price and a tragic end.

Try not to rejoice or gloat when you see others learn humility the hard way. Develop an attitude of humility like Mordecai and take care of your own pride, or you may be subject to the same lesson Haman learned.

Express It

Take a few moments to think of how you might serve someone this week, and resolve before God to do it. Then, thank God for the opportunity to reflect His goodness to the world around you.

Consider It

As you read Esther 6:1–13, consider these questions:

1) What did the king discover about Mordecai, and what would Mordecai's action have conveyed to the king?

____

____

2) Is there someone who has done something to help you whom you have not acknowledged? How can you honor him or her now?

____

____

3) Explain in your own words how Haman's pride winds up hurting him in Esther 6.

____

____

4) How has your self-centeredness hurt you in the past?

____

____

5) Review verses 8–9. Make a list of the steps Haman was to complete to honor Mordecai.

____

____

6) What would be done today to honor someone in a similar way?

____

____

7) Where did Mordecai go after he was honored?

____

____

8) Haman returned home with his head covered. What comments did his wife and friends make about his situation in verse 13?

____

____

Courage for Dinner

It's not always easy to see the bigger picture. We usually see how a situation (an edict or proclamation in Esther's case) will affect us personally, but understanding the larger issue isn't always as clear. As you see Esther's faith and courage in working to save her people, ask yourself if there is a situation in your life that just may be bigger than you are. Then ask God to use you to make a difference.

Esther 6:14–7:10

> ## *Key Verse*
>
> *Then Queen Esther answered, "If I have found favor in your sight, O king, and if it please the king, let my life be granted me for my wish, and my people for my request"* (Esther 7:3).

Esther Reveals Haman's Plot

14While they were yet talking with him,
the king's eunuchs arrived and hurried to
bring Haman to the feast that Esther had
prepared.

Haman Plans to Hang Mordecai

7 So the king and Haman went in to feast
with Queen Esther. 2And on the second
day, as they were drinking wine after
the feast, the king again said to Esther,
"What is your wish, Queen Esther? It
shall be granted you. And what is your
request? Even to the half of my kingdom,
it shall be fulfilled." 3Then Queen Esther
answered, "If I have found favor in your
sight, O king, and if it please the king,
let my life be granted me for my wish,
and my people for my request. 4For we
have been sold, I and my people, to
be destroyed, to be killed, and to be
annihilated. If we had been sold merely
as slaves, men and women, I would have
been silent, for our affliction is not to
be compared with the loss to the king."
5Then King Ahasuerus said to Queen
Esther, "Who is he, and where is he, who
has dared to do this?" 6And Esther said,
"A foe and enemy! This wicked Haman!"
Then Haman was terrified before the king
and the queen.

Haman Is Hanged

7And the king arose in his wrath from
the wine-drinking and went into the
palace garden, but Haman stayed to
beg for his life from Queen Esther,
for he saw that harm was determined
against him by the king. 8And the king
returned from the palace garden to the
place where they were drinking wine, as
Haman was falling on the couch where
Esther was. And the king said, "Will he
even assault the queen in my presence,
in my own house?" As the word left
the mouth of the king, they covered
Haman's face. 9Then Harbona, one of
the eunuchs in attendance on the king,
said, "Moreover, the gallows that Haman
has prepared for Mordecai, whose word
saved the king, is standing at Haman's
house, fifty cubits high." 10And the
king said, "Hang him on that." So they
hanged Haman on the gallows that he
had prepared for Mordecai. Then the
wrath of the king abated.

Go Deeper

There's something very natural and human about wanting revenge. The problem is, it is also very wrong. It reflects the worst in us. It violates God's will as well as His plan. God's will is not for us to take revenge on someone. God's plan is to allow Him to deal with those who try to harm us. "Beloved, never avenge yourselves, but leave it to the wrath of God, for it is written, 'Vengeance is mine, I will repay, says the Lord'" (Rom. 12:19).

But how do we deal with vengeful feelings? We deal with them the same way we deal with any of our sinful feelings. We have to admit that they are there and that we're not above that sort of thing. Beyond that, we have to recognize that indeed those kinds of feelings are sin. They're natural, but we're by nature sinners; therefore, they're sinful. So, we respond to those feelings the way we respond to any sin. We confess them as sin. We forsake them as sin.

Is there a lesson for us in the story of Haman? There sure is. This whole story is a clear example that when we take matters into our own hands and try to avenge ourselves, the end result is usually disastrous. It's the lesson of Galatians 6:7: "Do not be deceived: God is not mocked, for whatever one sows, that will he also reap." Haman hated the Jewish people and wanted revenge against Mordecai. He sowed revenge, yet revenge came home to roost. Revenge always does more damage to the one giving it than to the one receiving it.

Whatever you do, avoid revenge. You need to avoid taking revenge on an unappreciative boss, an unkind relative, or an unjust authority figure. Don't let your anger toward that person cause you to seek revenge. You need to avoid taking revenge on a pastor who doesn't do things exactly the way you think he ought. You need to avoid taking revenge on a wife who nags you about everything. Taking revenge is not God's plan for your life. "For we know him who said, 'Vengeance is mine; I will repay.' And again, 'The Lord will judge his people.' It is a fearful thing to fall into the hands of the living God" (Heb. 10:30–31). Let God deal with getting even, and you can be assured it'll be done right.

"Welcome to the queen's banquet. What would you like tonight? A generous courage steak, cooked to perfection and seasoned with care? Or a dish of abject desperation? How about a salad of humiliation with royal rage for dressing?"

If those serving at Esther's banquet had known what was about to happen, that would have been an appropriate menu to offer the puzzled king, a puffed-up prime minister and a purposeful queen.

"Esther needed courage to face the king. Nothing guaranteed that Ahasuerus would grant her request, despite his generous offers of half the kingdom. It was very possible that he would banish her in a rage just as he did Vashti."

It's a very dramatic scene as Esther takes center stage and exposes Haman's vicious plot against her and her people.

King Ahasuerus was intrigued and puzzled by the back-to-back invitations from his queen. Clearly Esther wanted something, and it had to be significant if she was willing to risk her neck for it. He asked first for her wish. (What would make her happy?) Then he asked for her request. (What is her agenda or deep desire?) It's interesting that he asked on two levels. One reflected something merely personal, a trifling thing, a treat, something to make her smile. The other pursued a deeper desire, the heart of her agenda, the stronger motivation for her actions. It's like offering your beloved a rose or a diamond. One is momentary, pleasant but short-lived. The other is long-term, committed, and costly.

Look at Esther's response: "If I have found favor in your sight, O king, and if it please the king, let my life be granted me for my wish, and my people for my request" (Esther 7:3). Her wish was to have her life spared and her request or desire was for her people. With these words Esther gave us a glimpse into her thought process. Her own life was a momentary, fleeting thing. Yes, it was valuable to her; but in the grand scheme of things, in the sovereign plan of God, the real treasure was the preservation of her people. This is really the heart of Esther's courage; she was willing to step up and speak out for her people because she believed it was more important for God's people to survive than for her to enjoy her own privileged life.

In fact, Esther went on to explain that if it was simply a matter of slavery, being traded like cattle in the marketplace, "I would have been silent, for our affliction is not to be compared with the loss to the king" (7:4). Instead, they were facing annihilation.

By the silent grace of God, Ahasuerus responded with outrage, not at Esther's boldness but at the diabolical plot against her and her people. When he demanded to know the perpetrator, Esther pointed to Haman, who must have listened to them in terror.

Click on your sympathy button for a moment and consider poor Haman. He had a hard day. It started early when he sought the king's permission to get rid of Mordecai, the thorn on his rose of proud privilege and position. Instead, Haman ended up taking Mordecai all over town, proclaiming the king's honor for this man he despised and hated.

Then his private dinner with the royal couple had turned into a complete nightmare. In his hatred of Mordecai, he had set in motion a plan that would also kill the queen, something that doesn't usually sit well with a king, no matter how much privilege and power an official has. Haman, once so puffed up with pride, was reduced to begging and blubbering for his life. To top it all off, the king mistook his miserable pleading for an assault on Esther!

It was the last straw for Ahasuerus and the end of the line for Haman. The servants covered his face (v. 8) as an indication that Haman was essentially a dead man. Another servant recalled the gallows prepared for Mordecai, and they were now used to execute Haman.

Haman's tragic end may appeal to our sense of justice, but it also serves as a powerful warning. Pride does go before a fall; the higher you rise in your own estimation, the greater the pain and struggle when you're brought low. God takes down the wicked and proud man in His own perfect timing. Haman's fate demonstrates that pride combined with hatred can be deadly, and we pay a heavier price than those we hate. When we hang on to our self-importance, our sense of superiority, and our prejudices, there is collateral damage to our spouses, children, and our work relationships. It can ruin a career or reputation, bring down a business, and undermine a ministry.

Along with these terrible warnings, chapter 7 also presents a profile in courage. Esther put everything on the line: her position, her privileged lifestyle, and most especially, her life.

Esther needed courage to face the king. Nothing guaranteed that Ahasuerus would grant her request, despite his generous offers of half the kingdom. It was very possible that he would banish her in a rage just as he did Vashti.

It also took courage for Esther to face the enemy. After all, to accuse Haman of this treachery when he was the king's favored right-hand man was a daring act. If the king stood by Haman as his trusted advisor, she would be no match for their power.

Esther demonstrated courage, too, as she stood up for her people and sided with them. As queen of the empire, for Esther to identify with a group of conquered exiles could have been perceived as disloyalty to the king, even treasonous. She didn't know how the king would react to learning she was a Jew. For all she knew, he was just as eager as Haman to exterminate her people.

When you stack up all the unknowns Esther faced that evening, her courage becomes even more remarkable. God gives His people His grace and power when they choose to act with righteous courage. Courage is rooted in the confidence that, no matter what, God will bring about what is good and right. So, when the Lord calls you to step up, when He gives you an opportunity to speak out, "Be strong and courageous. Do not be frightened, and do not be dismayed, for the Lord your God is with you wherever you go" (Josh. 1:9).

Express It

List the character qualities you have seen in Esther so far. Which of those would you most like to possess? Write five action steps you can take this week to demonstrate that quality in your life.

Consider It

As you read Esther 6:14–7:10, consider these questions:

1) Think about the two questions Ahasuerus asked Queen Esther. What do these reveal about the king?

2) How do the king's questions remind you of God's love for you?

3) Esther asked for deliverance rather than revenge. What does this reveal about her?

4) To whom did Haman plead when he asked for his life to be spared?

5) List the examples of justice and mercy you find in this chapter.

6) What emotion did King Ahasuerus exhibit here that we have seen previously? When was this emotion first seen in the story?

7) In your own words, what information did Harbona present to the king?

8) This was the second time in one day Haman's head was covered. What are the differences in the covering? (See Esther 6:12 and 7:8.)

Finishing the Job

Esther is an amazing story of God's sovereign hand of protection for His chosen people. He gives you the same protection over your enemies. As you study this passage, think about the privileges God has given you as one of His people.

Esther 8:1–9:19

Esther Saves the Jews

8 On that day King Ahasuerus gave to Queen Esther the house of Haman, the enemy of the Jews. And Mordecai came before the king, for Esther had told what he was to her. 2And the king took off his signet ring, which he had taken from Haman, and gave it to Mordecai. And Esther set Mordecai over the house of Haman.

3Then Esther spoke again to the king. She fell at his feet and wept and pleaded with him to avert the evil plan of Haman the Agagite and the plot that he had devised against the Jews. 4When the king held out the golden scepter to Esther, 5Esther rose and stood before the king. And she said, "If it please the king, and if I have found favor in his sight, and if the thing seems right before the king, and I am pleasing in his eyes, let an order be written to revoke the letters devised by Haman the Agagite, the son of Hammedatha, which he wrote to destroy the Jews who are in all the provinces of the king. 6For how can I bear to see the calamity that is coming to my people? Or how can I bear to see the destruction of my kindred?" 7Then King Ahasuerus said to Queen Esther and to Mordecai the Jew, "Behold, I have given Esther the house of Haman, and they have hanged him on the gallows, because he intended to lay hands on the Jews. 8But you may write as you please with regard to the Jews, in the name of the king, and seal it with the king's ring, for an edict written in the name of the king and sealed with the king's ring cannot be revoked."

9The king's scribes were summoned at that time, in the third month, which is the month of Sivan, on the twenty-third day. And an edict was written, according to all that Mordecai commanded concerning the Jews, to the satraps and the governors and the officials of the provinces from India to Ethiopia, 127 provinces, to each province in its own script and to each people in its own language, and also to the Jews in their script and their language. 10And he wrote in the name of King Ahasuerus and sealed it with the king's signet ring. Then he sent the letters by mounted couriers riding on swift horses that were used in the king's service, bred from the royal stud, 11saying that the king allowed the Jews who were in every city to gather and defend their lives, to destroy, to kill, and to annihilate any armed force of any people or province that might attack them, children and women included, and to plunder their goods, 12on one day throughout all the provinces of King Ahasuerus, on the thirteenth day of the twelfth month, which is the month of

Key Verse

Now in the twelfth month, which is the month of Adar, on the thirteenth day of the same, when the king's command and edict were about to be carried out, on the very day when the enemies of the Jews hoped to gain the mastery over them, the reverse occurred: the Jews gained mastery over those who hated them. The Jews gathered in their cities throughout all the provinces of King Ahasuerus to lay hands on those who sought their harm. And no one could stand against them, for the fear of them had fallen on all peoples (Esther 9:1–2).

Adar. [13]A copy of what was written was to be issued as a decree in every province, being publicly displayed to all peoples, and the Jews were to be ready on that day to take vengeance on their enemies. [14]So the couriers, mounted on their swift horses that were used in the king's service, rode out hurriedly, urged by the king's command. And the decree was issued in Susa the citadel.

[15]Then Mordecai went out from the presence of the king in royal robes of blue and white, with a great golden crown and a robe of fine linen and purple, and the city of Susa shouted and rejoiced. [16]The Jews had light and gladness and joy and honor. [17]And in every province and in every city, wherever the king's command and his edict reached, there was gladness and joy among the Jews, a feast and a holiday. And many from the peoples of the country declared themselves Jews, for fear of the Jews had fallen on them.

The Jews Destroy Their Enemies

9 Now in the twelfth month, which is the month of Adar, on the thirteenth day of the same, when the king's command and edict were about to be carried out, on the very day when the enemies of the Jews hoped to gain the mastery over them, the reverse occurred: the Jews gained mastery over those who hated them. [2]The Jews gathered in their cities throughout all the provinces of King Ahasuerus to lay hands on those who sought their harm. And no one could stand against them, for the fear of them had fallen on all peoples. [3]All the officials of the provinces and the satraps and the governors and the royal agents also helped the Jews, for the fear of Mordecai had fallen on them. [4]For Mordecai was great in the king's house, and his fame spread throughout all the provinces, for the man Mordecai grew more and more powerful. [5]The Jews struck all their enemies with the sword, killing and destroying them, and did as they pleased to those who hated them. [6]In Susa the citadel itself the Jews killed and destroyed 500 men, [7]and also killed Parshandatha and Dalphon and Aspatha [8]and Poratha and Adalia and Aridatha [9]and Parmashta and Arisai and Aridai and Vaizatha, [10]the ten sons of Haman the son of Hammedatha, the enemy of the Jews, but they laid no hand on the plunder.

[11]That very day the number of those killed in Susa the citadel was reported to the king. [12]And the king said to Queen Esther, "In Susa the citadel the Jews have killed and destroyed 500 men and also the ten sons of Haman. What then have they done in the rest of the king's provinces! Now what is your wish? It shall be granted you. And what further is your request? It shall be fulfilled." [13]And Esther said, "If it please the king, let the Jews who are in Susa be allowed tomorrow also to do according to this day's edict. And let the ten sons of Haman be hanged on the gallows." [14]So the king commanded this to be done. A decree was issued in Susa, and the ten sons of Haman were hanged. [15]The Jews who were in Susa gathered also on the fourteenth day of the month of Adar and they killed 300 men in Susa, but they laid no hands on the plunder.

[16]Now the rest of the Jews who were in the king's provinces also gathered to defend their lives, and got relief from their enemies and killed 75,000 of those who hated them, but they laid no hands on the plunder. [17]This was on the thirteenth day of the month of Adar, and on the fourteenth day they rested and made that a day of feasting and gladness. [18]But the Jews who were in Susa gathered on the thirteenth day and on the fourteenth, and rested on the fifteenth day, making that a day of feasting and gladness. [19]Therefore the Jews of the villages, who live in the rural towns, hold the fourteenth day of the month of Adar as a day for gladness and feasting, as a holiday, and as a day on which they send gifts of food to one another.

Go Deeper

It's encouraging to see how, despite the conspiracies of those in positions of power and the spiritual forces of the enemy, God protects His people. All you have to do is read through the pages of history, and you'll find that again and again great nations have attempted to destroy the Jewish people: the Syrians, the Assyrians, the Egyptians and even Nazi Germany. Yet the Jews have survived every effort to annihilate them.

Anti-Semitism is an evil that is still present in the world today. Yet God's promises are also still present too. Isaiah 54:17 declares, "No weapon that is fashioned against you shall succeed, and you shall confute every tongue that rises against you in judgment. This is the heritage of the servants of the Lord and their vindication from me, declares the Lord."

This promise was true in the days of Mordecai and Haman. It was true in the days of Hitler. It is true today. God is doing the same thing for those of us who are not Jewish but who belong to Him. We can see the preservation of the Church around the world even though more believers are being martyred today than ever before. But where persecution exists, God's grace persists even more and His remnant of followers is protected. God keeps His promises to us as He did for Israel.

It always happens, doesn't it? Solve one problem and another crops up. The story of Esther is no exception. When Esther 7 closes with the death of Haman after his conspiracy against the Jews is exposed, King Ahasuerus exacts swift justice. It's all over, right?

Not quite. There's still the matter of the royal edict against the Jews. And there is no way to reverse the decree. If the Persian Empire didn't invent the term "written in stone," they certainly perfected it. Any order or law issued with the king's seal was irrevocable, impossible to overturn. It could not be adjusted or overthrown. So, while the king acted on Esther's plea for her life and her people by executing Haman (Esther 7:3–4), there was still a law on the books that meant the extermination of any Jews throughout the empire.

Before dealing with this problem, let's examine the immediate fallout from Haman's hasty death. Since he was executed as a

"Each step along the way, God silently placed Mordecai and Esther into key positions in order to preserve His people."

criminal, everything Haman owned became the property of the crown. It pleased Ahasuerus to give it all—the house, the land, all the attendants, all the treasures—to Esther. When she brought up her relationship with Mordecai (8:1–2), the king immediately gave his signet ring to Mordecai. This had belonged to Haman, but the king reclaimed it and awarded it to Mordecai with all the rights and responsibilities of prime minister.

Everything that Haman had been proud of and worked to achieve now belonged to the man he hated the most. Nothing was left of his wealth or power; even his family was about to be wiped out. (9:6–10,14).

Each step along the way, God silently placed Mordecai and Esther into key positions in order to preserve His people. Mordecai is now elevated to second-in-command and the administrator of a great estate (once Haman's) as well as the greatest empire of his day.

Then Esther came back to the king in Esther 8:3 to tackle one last problem. All the mischief that Haman had decreed against the Jews needed to be reversed. The king held out the golden scepter to her again, indicating that he was willing not only to receive Esther but to listen to her.

It took courage for Esther to come again and request Ahasuerus to reverse the decree. Before she got down to business, Esther was careful and wise in presenting her appeal. "And she said, 'If it please the king, and if I have found favor in his sight, and if the thing seems right before the king, and I am pleasing in his eyes'" (8:5). She understood a few things about how to persuade and gain favor with those in power. Although she was clearly favored at this point, she had enough wisdom not to just barge into the king's presence and demand that he do something about her need.

It seemed like a simple request: A second decree needed to be written and sent out that would override the first decree. However, she was asking the king to reverse the irreversible. Remember, it was impossible to change a royal decree, even if you were the king. Ahasuerus, however, offered a solution: give Mordecai, now the prime minister, permission to write a second decree and put the royal seal on it, giving it equal authority to the first.

With God-given wisdom, Mordecai created a second decree "saying that the king allowed the Jews who were in every city to gather and defend their lives, to destroy, to kill, and to annihilate any armed force of any people or province that might attack them, children and women included, and to plunder their goods, on one day throughout all the provinces of King Ahasuerus, on the thirteenth day of the twelfth month, which is the month of Adar" (vv. 11–12).

The Jews were given permission to fight back and defend themselves against their enemies. They were given a day of vengeance; they did not have to take it lying down. The decree included retribution. Not only could the Jews defend themselves, they also could "destroy, kill, and annihilate any armed force of any people or province that might attack them." It also said they could claim the spoils of those they destroyed, although, when the day came, they did not exercise this right (9:16). As the good news of this new edict reached God's people, they turned the day into one of celebration (8:15–17).

Then the day established by the edicts arrived and chapter 9 records the results. "On the very day when the enemies of the Jews hoped to gain the mastery over them, the reverse occurred: the Jews gained mastery over those who hated them. The Jews gathered in their cities throughout all the provinces of King Ahasuerus to lay hands on those who sought their harm. And no one could stand against them, for the fear of them had fallen on all peoples" (9:1–2). Many leaders under Ahasuerus became allies of Mordecai and the Jews because they feared Mordecai—and Mordecai's God.

Oh yes, God is present in the Book of Esther. Even if He is not named, He was the one celebrated and glorified by His people at the end of chapter 8. He was the one who gave wisdom and courage to Mordecai and Esther. And it was His power at work that the people of the empire feared. Many even identified themselves with the Jews (8:17) because God's good hand was upon His people.

God moved in His grace, and He saved His people even as they faced death by decree. This was more than just a plot by some narrow-minded court official with a heart full of hate. Haman was only a tool in Satan's ongoing attempt to destroy the people of God. In effect, it was an attack upon God Himself. That's why God allowed the Jews to avenge themselves. What could have been a disaster became instead a stage upon which God could demonstrate His superiority. This was God's way of preserving His chosen people.

That hasn't changed. There is a God who loves us. There is a God who cares for us. There is a God who is involved in our daily lives. That's certainly borne out in the story of Esther and Mordecai.

Express It

This week, keep a daily journal of how you have seen God's involvement in your life. Be sure to look for small, seemingly unimportant details that communicate God's care for you as well as His provision in the larger events of your life.

Consider It

As you read Esther 8:1–9:19, consider these questions:

1) Which of Esther's requests had evidently NOT been taken care of in chapter 7?

2) Make a list of the gifts given in Esther 8:1–2, and note who received each gift.

3) How is Esther's request in verses 3–6 different from her request in Esther 7:3? What are some possible reasons for the change?

4) Examine the king's response to Esther. What does it reveal about his attitude toward his queen?

5) Compare Esther 3:1–4:3 with Esther 8:1–17. What are the similarities and differences in these two situations?

6) Consider the fact that the Jewish people "laid no hand on the plunder" (9:10). This fact is restated twice in verses 15 and 16. Why is this so important to note?

7) According to verse 9:19, how do the Jews celebrate Purim?

A Time to Celebrate

Many times, we get so wrapped up in the next thing we need to do that we forget to celebrate what God has just done for us. As you conclude your study of Esther and God's grace in her life and the lives of her people, schedule a time for a little celebration of your own.

Esther 9:20–10:3

The Feast of Purim Inaugurated

[20]And Mordecai recorded these
things and sent letters to all the Jews
who were in all the provinces of King
Ahasuerus, both near and far, [21]obliging
them to keep the fourteenth day of
the month Adar and also the fifteenth
day of the same, year by year, [22]as the
days on which the Jews got relief from
their enemies, and as the month that
had been turned for them from sorrow
into gladness and from mourning into
a holiday; that they should make them
days of feasting and gladness, days for
sending gifts of food to one another and
gifts to the poor.

[23]So the Jews accepted what they had
started to do, and what Mordecai had
written to them. [24]For Haman the Agagite,
the son of Hammedatha, the enemy of
all the Jews, had plotted against the Jews
to destroy them, and had cast Pur (that
is, cast lots), to crush and to destroy
them. [25]But when it came before the
king, he gave orders in writing that his
evil plan that he had devised against
the Jews should return on his own
head, and that he and his sons should
be hanged on the gallows. [26]Therefore
they called these days Purim, after the
term Pur. Therefore, because of all that
was written in this letter, and of what
they had faced in this matter, and of
what had happened to them, [27]the Jews
firmly obligated themselves and their
offspring and all who joined them, that
without fail they would keep these two
days according to what was written and
at the time appointed every year, [28]that
these days should be remembered and
kept throughout every generation, in
every clan, province, and city, and that
these days of Purim should never fall
into disuse among the Jews, nor should
the commemoration of these days cease
among their descendants.

Key Verse

And Mordecai recorded these things and sent letters to all the Jews who were in all the provinces of King Ahasuerus, both near and far, obliging them to keep the fourteenth day of the month Adar and also the fifteenth day of the same, year by year, as the days on which the Jews got relief from their enemies, and as the month that had been turned for them from sorrow into gladness and from mourning into a holiday; that they should make them days of feasting and gladness, days for sending gifts of food to one another and gifts to the poor (Esther 9:20–22).

[29]Then Queen Esther, the daughter of
Abihail, and Mordecai the Jew gave full
written authority, confirming this second
letter about Purim. [30]Letters were sent
to all the Jews, to the 127 provinces of
the kingdom of Ahasuerus, in words
of peace and truth, [31]that these days
of Purim should be observed at their
appointed seasons, as Mordecai the Jew
and Queen Esther obligated them, and
as they had obligated themselves and

their offspring, with regard to their fasts and their lamenting. [32]The command of Queen Esther confirmed these practices of Purim, and it was recorded in writing.

The Greatness of Mordecai

10 King Ahasuerus imposed tax on
the land and on the coastlands of the
sea. [2]And all the acts of his power and
might, and the full account of the high
honor of Mordecai, to which the king
advanced him, are they not written in
the Book of the Chronicles of the kings
of Media and Persia? [3]For Mordecai
the Jew was second in rank to King
Ahasuerus, and he was great among the
Jews and popular with the multitude of
his brothers, for he sought the welfare
of his people and spoke peace to all his
people.

Go Deeper

Esther is clearly the heroine in this story. But in this final chapter and verse, it is Mordecai's greatness that is exclaimed. Notice some things about the greatness of this man.

First, he is great because he is second only to the king. "For Mordecai the Jew was second in rank to King Ahasuerus" (Esther 10:3). To be second to the king of the Persian Empire meant that you were revered throughout the entire empire. Being second to the king meant that Mordecai was the right-hand man of a very powerful king. Remember the preceding chapter. It says, "All the officials of the provinces and the satraps and the governors and the royal agents also helped the Jews, for the fear of Mordecai had fallen on them" (9:3).

But the second half of 10:3 tells us the real greatness of Mordecai: "He was great among the Jews and popular with the multitude of his brothers, for he sought the welfare of his people and spoke peace to all his people." He was a great example to the Jews of faithfulness. Remember, Mordecai was the fellow who would not bow to Haman. He chose to put his life on the line rather than dishonor his God.

In addition, Mordecai was a man who sought the welfare of his people, the Jews. Mordecai's public life and service in government was for the benefit of his people, not to line his own pockets.

Finally, he was a man who was speaking peace to all his people. He was securing for them a quiet and peaceful existence. He was seeking the kind of peace that arises from a sense of justice, that he'd done the right thing. He was seeking the kind of social peace that prevails when more than one race inhabits a society. Mordecai was great among his people not because he sought greatness, but because he pursued the welfare and peace of his people.

As Christians, God is interested in how we serve Him as well. God wants us to be like Mordecai—to seek good for people, to be men and women of principle, to refuse to bow to anyone or anything other than the One True God.

When the struggle is over and the victory is yours, it's time to celebrate. When you want to mark a milestone or achievement, you throw a party. When you want to remember God's goodness in your life, you share it with your friends and family.

The Book of Esther closes with a celebration like that. Victory, achievement, and the good grace of God all contributed to this new feast called Purim. God's people, scattered through the Persian Empire, faced death, but now they had a reason to rejoice. In Esther 9:1–18, we saw how the Jews overcame those who sought to destroy them under Haman's edict. So, a celebration was completely in order.

By order of the new prime minister, Mordecai, and under the authority of the king, a new feast was proclaimed to celebrate "the days on which the Jews got relief from their enemies, and as the month that had been turned for them from sorrow into gladness and from mourning into a holiday" (Esther 9:22). It became the feast of Purim, a reference to the *Pur* or lots that Haman cast in order to choose the day for the Jews' destruction. Jewish people around the world still gather to celebrate this feast and remember how God protects and delivers His people.

While you may not be Jewish or celebrate the feast of Purim, it still reminds us all of reasons to rejoice. First, it reflects on the sovereignty of God. God protects His people even today. He is present at all times, even if we don't hear directly from Him. When He says, "Behold, I am with you always" (Matt. 28:20), you can trust that promise. The power of kings and the plans of hate-filled people can't diminish the sovereignty of God. The Jewish people must have wondered, *Where is God?* when they were under the sentence of death by Haman. But God was still in control even if it's not obvious. (See Ps. 115:3.)

Purim also teaches us the value of remembering what God has done, remembering how the Lord preserved His people in the midst of great trial and that He does the same thing today. He rescues the helpless; He redeems the lost and enslaved; and He offers life and hope to those who are spiritually dead and hopeless.

We have a tendency to forget God's goodness and only remember

> *"Remember how the Lord preserved His people in the midst of great trial and that He does the same thing today. He rescues the helpless; He redeems the lost and enslaved; and He offers life and hope to those who are spiritually dead and hopeless."*

the tragedies of life that we can't explain. Purim teaches us to remember that God is good, all the time. It also offers insight into community: we need each other not only to share our sorrows but to celebrate our victories as well. Coming together increases our joy as we understand what the Lord has done for us.

God may not be mentioned by name in the Book of Esther, but His fingerprints are all over this story. His tools are two people (Esther and Mordecai) who are also worth celebrating for the examples they give to us of courage, wisdom, watchfulness, and faith.

Esther teaches us the value of humility in a place of power; she didn't fight and scratch to get to the top; she didn't abuse her position or seek self-promotion. Instead she was willing to be a servant of God, willing to step forward with courage at "such a time as this." She knew the wisdom of preparation and persuasion in bringing the truth to light. Her Hebrew name, *Hadassah*, means "star," and Esther was a shining star of courage even when it could have cost her life.

Mordecai is the other hero of the Book of Esther. Esther 10 gives us a glimpse into what he accomplished as a prime minister. His reputation is summed up in 10:3: "He was great among the Jews and popular with the multitude of his brothers, for he sought the welfare of his people and spoke peace to all his people." Not bad for a man who previously spent his days sitting at the gates of the palace, waiting and watching. Mordecai was a great example of humility. He didn't seek glory, but when the position of greatness came to him, he handled it wisely.

Mordecai was also a man of honor who sought to do what was right, even if it made him unpopular (3:1–5). He didn't complain when he didn't get credit for his good deeds (2:19–23), but in God's perfect timing, this faithful and righteous man received a great reward. Mordecai never forgot his loyalty to his people and to God. Even when pushing Esther to take a stand, he referred to his belief that God would deliver (4:14). And when placed in a position of great power and influence, Mordecai still sought to do what was best for his people.

From the very beginning, Mordecai was watching over other people. He took Esther in when she was orphaned and raised her as his own. He watched over her as she entered the king's household and took up his place at the gate when she became queen. He was her counsel and encouragement when the threat of Haman's edict became public. And in the end, Mordecai was in a position to watch over the welfare of his own people. Through his quiet example, Mordecai reminds us of God the Father who watches over us at every turn. He takes care of us; He counsels and encourages us as He calls on us to serve. While God may not be mentioned by name, the words and deeds of Mordecai give us a glimpse into His presence and actions on behalf of His people.

Like all good stories, the Book of Esther offers a happy ending with a celebration that includes the hero and heroine receiving the honor they deserved. But Esther is much more than a good story. Esther shows us the sovereign hand of God at work through those willing to trust Him with their lives. It reminds us of the value of humility and the dangers of pride, the hazards of pursuing our own agenda and the treasure we find when we willingly submit to God's plans. God is good, extending His grace and presence to us even when He is silent.

Express It

It's not hard to say we know God is taking care of us, but it is sometimes hard to believe it. Are you faced with an overwhelming challenge today? Remember that your Heavenly Father is watching over you at every turn. As you seek Him, He will counsel and encourage you in just the right way at just the right time. Take some time right now to remember and celebrate God's faithful provision in your life. Then take some time to share His faithfulness with someone else who needs to know His presence.

Consider It

As you read Esther 9:20–10:3, consider these questions:

1) Why were the Jews directed to celebrate Purim every year?

2) What three things were they to do on Purim? What might these three acts have represented to the people?

3) Compare the tradition of casting *Pur* with the constant faithfulness of God displayed throughout the Book of Esther.

4) In verses 27 and 28, what did the Jews "firmly obligate" themselves to do?

5) Why was the feast to be celebrated on two days instead of one?

6) Refer to chapter 10, verse 3, and note why Mordecai was "great" and "popular" among his people.

7) How did you see those characteristics displayed in Mordecai's words and deeds?

Notes

Notes